quick crochet

Quick Crochet

35 fast, fun projects to make in a weekend

Chrissie Day

CICO BOOKS

LONDON NEW YORK

Published in 2007 by CICO Books
an imprint of Ryland Peters & Small
519 Broadway, 5th Floor, New York, NY 10012

www.cicobooks.co.uk

10 9 8 7 6 5 4 3 2 1

A CIP catalog record for this book is available from the
Library of Congress

ISBN-13: 978 1 904991 93 9
ISBN-10: 1 904991 93 9

Printed in China

Editor: Marie Clayton
Designer: Roger Hammond
Photographers: Paul Bricknall, Geoff Dann and Tino Tedaldi

contents

introduction

In an age of high technology it is refreshing to know that one of the oldest crafts—crochet—has not only survived but has a fresh new following wanting to learn and explore. I have crocheted for about as long as I have knitted and, in this world where speed is essential, it seems comforting to know that crochet work is quicker than knitting. Once the basics have been mastered, "the sky's the limit" as new textures, new patterns beckon you to try, as well as all the possible materials: cottons, linens, raffia, leather, wire, silks. Whether you are making a piece in fine cotton or silk or using chunky wool, the stitch is the same and it is the same language in any country— crochet is universal.

As always, each piece starts as a sketch—an idea in my sketch book—and it is only when I have finished this process that it is taken further as yarn is introduced and the decision taken that a crochet stitch is needed for the item. In this book you will find differing projects, which I hope will excite you and hasten you to get out your hook and give it a try. Choice of colors and yarns is always hard and I hope the colors I have chosen in this book inspire you—but do not be afraid to do these designs in other colorways. Color is personal, so never be afraid to change what you see on the page to a color that suits you or that you like better.

I love experimenting by adding other fibers and pushing the medium by combining other materials and techniques in unusual ways. Think outside the box and invent your own ways to use these patterns with differing textures. Crochet is addictive, yet calming, and will help you be at one with the ups and downs of life—let it into your life and enjoy the journey!

I think if my stitches were tears I would have crocheted an ocean by now, but equally much of my work is interlaced with love and soft memories—the golden times of the present and the past worked into every stitch, binding the garment together. I dedicate this book to all those who have ever taught me and shown me the way.

hats, wraps, and gloves

The right hat, wrap, or pair of gloves in a pleasing yarn that suits the wearer does so much more than just enhance an outfit. The projects in this chapter include a range of very different hats, some wonderfully textured scarves and wraps, a luxurious shrug, sparkly arm warmers, and a pretty pair of lacy gloves.

A hat denotes your mood of the moment—which can change as much as you want it to! Feel glamorous in the soft Cashmere Helmet that fits closely to your head, or bring back memories of the Bloomsbury set with the Silky Cloche Hat. Crochet lends itself to creating wonderful textures and these have been my starting point for many of the projects in this book. The Curlique-end Scarf has cascades of twists at each end, while the Bobble Hat is a riot of texture all over.

The wonderful yarns now on offer also offer constant inspiration—colors, textures, silk, alpaca, cashmere, merino—the variety available is almost endless. So express your creativity and enjoy the exciting projects on the following pages.

Materials
1 × 100g ball of Wensleydale DK, color 123, cerise (A)
1 × 100g ball of Wensleydale DK, color 154, aubergine (B)
E/4 (3.50 mm) crochet hook
Piece of cardboard to make the tassel
Yarn needle

Size
Approx 45 in. (115 cm) after felting.

Gauge
Gauge is not important on this project, as the finished piece will be felted.

Abbreviations
ch chain
cont continue
rep repeat
sc single crochet
ss slip stitch
st(s) stitch(es)

Special instructions
To felt the scarf, wash in very hot water with liquid soap, rubbing gently with your hands until the fibers begin to matt together. Alternatively you can put it in the washing machine, but it is less easy to control the process. The rings will become smaller and firmer when felted, but be careful they do not stick together. For more detailed felting instructions, see page 76.

chain link felted scarf with tassels

The dramatic colors and bold shapes of this unusual scarf will bring you attention wherever you go! I love the rounded shapes in chunky chains and I have used them here to create a light, open scarf that is fun to wear.

CIRCLE 1
Using A, make 35ch, ss into first ch to form a ring.
Round 1: 1ch, 1sc into same place as ss, 1sc into each ch, ss into first sc, turn.
Round 2: 1ch, 1sc into each sc, ss into first sc, turn.
Rep this last round twice more.
Fasten off.

CIRCLE 2
As circle 1, but thread commencing ch through circle 1 before joining into ring.

CIRCLES 3–6
Make and join 1 more A circle and 3 B circles, joining circle 6 to circle 1.

CIRCLES 7–8
Join 1 A circle to first B circle and 1 A circle to 3rd B circle.

CIRCLES 9–10
Join 1 A circle to circle 7 and 1 A circle to circle 8, linking each through center B circle.

CIRCLE 11
Join 1 A circle through both circles 9 and 10.

CIRCLE 12
Join 1 B circle through circles 9 and 11.

CIRCLE 13
Join 1 B circle through circles 10 and 11.

CIRCLE 14
Join 1 B circle through circles 11 and 12.

CIRCLE 15
Join 1 B circle through circles 11 and 13.

CIRCLE 16
Join 1 B circle through circles 14 and 15.

CIRCLE 17
Join 1 A circle through circle 14.

CIRCLE 18
Join 1 A circle through circle 15.
Continue in this way, changing color after every 5 circles, until work measures approx 44 in. (110 cm) ending with 1 circle linking 2 circles.

TASSEL
Using A and B, make a tassel 8¾ in. (22 cm) long. Stitch the tassel to one end of the scarf and loop the last chain of the other end over it.

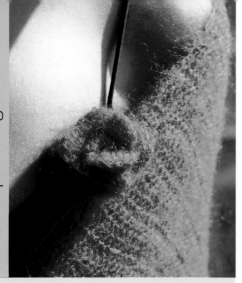

cerise rose shawl

A large stole trimmed with roses—a really pretty design for those warm summer evenings when you need romance in the air around you. The stole is made in three sections and the roses are used to join them for an open and light effect.

Materials
9 × 25g balls of Rowan Kidsilk Haze, candy girl (A)
1 × 25g ball of Rowan Kidsilk Haze, jelly (B)
E/4 (3.50 mm) crochet hook
Yarn needle

Size
36 × 58 in. (92 × 148 cm).

Gauge
16 sts and 9 rows to 4 in. (10 cm) over sc using E/4 (3.50 mm) hook.

Abbreviations
ch chain
ch sp chain space
dc double crochet
rem remaining
rep repeat
sc single crochet
st(s) stitch(es)

STOLE
(Make 3 identical sections)
Using A make 52ch.
Row 1: 1dc in 4th ch, 1dc in each ch to end. (50 sts)
Row 2: Ch3 (counts as dc), 1dc in each dc.
Rep Row 2 until 133 rows or 58 in. (148 cm) have been worked.
Fasten off.

ROSES
(Make a selection in 3 sizes and varying colors including some using 1 strand of each color together)
Using A, make 16 or 26 or 36ch.
Row 1: 1dc in 4th ch, *1ch, skip 1ch, (1dc, 1ch, 1dc) in next ch (V-stitch worked); rep until there are 6(11,16) V-sts.

Row 2: Ch3 (counts as dc), 5dc in first ch sp *1sc in next ch sp, 6dc in next ch sp, (shell stitch made); rep from * to end, 6dc in last ch sp. Fasten off, leaving a long tail. Thread onto a needle and take down to first row, roll up first ⅜ in. (1 cm) to form a bud, roll rest and stitch down.

MAKING UP
Fasten the three sections together with crocheted roses. Line all three pieces up side-by-side. Slightly overlapping the upper layer on each pin the two centers and attach a rose at each. Attach remaining roses at intervals, to join sections. Fold top section over center section and join top corners to lower corners of each center section to make holes for arms.

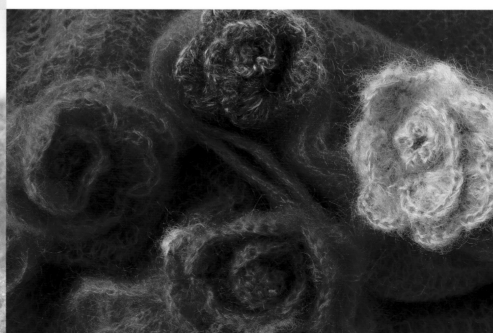

bobbles hat

Just wild bobbles everywhere on this funky and multicolored hat! You will create a stir wherever you go while wearing it. The yarn is dyed to create the multicolor effect, so no need to worry about color changes. The crown is topped with a cluster of loops for an unusual finishing touch.

Materials
3 x 50g balls of Twilleys Freedom, color 408
H/8 (5.00 mm) crochet hook
J/10 (6.00 mm) crochet hook

Size
One size, to fit average adult head.

Gauge
11 sts and 13 rounds to 4 in. (10 cm) over sc using J/10 (6.00 mm) crochet hook.

Abbreviations
bl back loop
ch chain
dc double crochet
RS right side
sc single crochet
ss slip stitch
st(s) stitch(es)
WS wrong side

Special abbreviations
MB—make bobble, always inserting the hook into the same st and leaving the last loop of each st on the hook, yarn over hook and draw through all the loops on the hook.

HAT

Using J/10 (6.00 mm) hook, make 3ch, into 3rd ch from hook work 6sc, ss into first sc of round, turn.

Round 1 (WS): 1ch, 2sc into each sc, ss into first sc, turn. (12 sc)

Round 2 (RS): 1ch, 2sc into each sc, ss into first sc of round, turn. (24 sc)

Round 3: 1ch, 1sc into each sc to end, ss into first sc, turn.

Round 4: 1ch, 1sc into each of first 2sc, [MB into next sc, 1sc into each of next 3sc] 5 times, MB into next sc, 1sc into last sc, ss into first sc, turn.

Round 5: 1ch, 1sc into first sc, [2sc into next sc, 1sc into next sc] to last sc, 2sc into last sc, ss into first sc, turn. (36 sc)

Round 6: 1ch, 1sc into each sc, ss into first sc, turn.

Round 7: 1ch, 1sc into each of first 2sc, 2sc into next sc, [1sc into each of next 2sc, 2sc into next sc] to end, ss into first sc, turn. (48 sc)

Round 8: As Round 6.

Round 9: 1ch, 1sc into each of first 3sc, 2sc into next sc, [1sc into each of next 3sc, 2sc into next sc] to end, ss into first sc, turn. (60 sc)

Round 10: As Round 5.

Round 11: 1ch, [1sc into each of next 9sc, 2sc into next sc] to end, ss into first sc, turn. (66 sc)

Round 12: 1ch, 1sc into each of first 5sc, [MB into next sc, 1sc into each of next 7sc] 7 times, MB into next sc, 1sc into each of last 4 sc, ss into first sc, turn.

Rounds 13–15: 1ch, 1sc into each sc, ss into first sc, turn.

Round 16: 1ch, 1sc into first sc, [MB into next sc, 1sc into each of next 7sc] 7 times, MB into next sc, 1sc into each of last 8 sc, ss into first sc, turn.

Rounds 17–19: As Rounds 13–15.

Rounds 20–23: As Rounds 12–15.

Do not fasten off.

Ribbing edge

Change to H/8 (5.00 mm) hook.

Row 1: 5ch, 1sc into 2nd ch from hook, 1sc into each of 3ch, ss into next st of last round of hat body. (4 sc)

Row 2: Working into the bl only, 1sc into each of next 4 sc, turn.

Row 3: Still working into bl only, 1ch, 1sc into each of 4 sc, ss into each of next 2 sts of last row of hat, turn.

Rep Rows 2 and 3 until ribbing meets up to first row of rib.

On last row of ribbing, work through the bl and the opposite side of the foundation ch of the ribbing, ss into each of the 4 sc.

Fasten off.

MAKING UP

With RS of hat facing and H/8 (5.00 mm) hook, join yarn to any sc of base row of hat, working round the top center circle, [12ch, ss into next sc of circle] 5 times, 12ch, ss into first ss.

This forms a group of 6 loops into top circle of hat.

Fasten off.

hats, wraps and gloves

Materials
4 x 50g balls of Colinette Cadenza, marble
H/8 (5.00 mm) crochet hook

Size
Length 30¾ in. (78 cm); width 6 in. (15 cm).

Gauge
19 sc and 20 rows to 4 in. (10 cm) over sc
using H/8 (5.00 mm) hook.

Abbreviations
ch chain
dc double crochet
rep repeat
RS right side
sc single crochet
ss slip stitch
st(s) stitch(es)
WS wrong side
yoh yarn over hook

Special abbreviations
MB—make bobble, leaving last loop of
each dc on hook, work 7dc in same st, yoh
and draw through all the loops on the
hook. Push bobble through to RS.

curlicue-end scarf

I love texture, and here I have combined bobble with the
twisted shapes of curlicues. Although it looks quite complex,
this scarf is not that difficult to make—just remember to push
the bobbles to the right side as they are made.

MAIN SECTION
Make 29ch.
Base row (RS): 1sc into 2nd ch from
hook, 1sc into each ch to end. (28 sc)
Row 1: 1ch, 1sc into each sc to end,
turn.
Rep last row until scarf measures
17 in. (43 cm), ending with a WS
row. Do not fasten off.
With RS of main section of scarf
facing, make 31ch.
Curlicue ends
Base row: 1dc into 4th ch from
hook, 1dc into each ch to end, turn.
(29 sts)
Row 1 (WS): 1ch, 1sc into first 2dc,
*MB into next dc, 1sc into each of
next 3dc; rep from * to last 3sts, MB
into next dc, 1sc into next dc, 1sc
into top of 3ch, turn.
Row 2: 3ch (count as 1dc), skip first
sc, 1dc into each st to end.
Row 3: 1ch, 1sc into first 4dc, *MB,
1sc into each of next 3dc; rep from *
to last st, 1sc into top of 3ch, turn.
Row 4: As Row 2.
Rep Rows 1–4, ss in other corner of
main section.
Fasten off.

Making tucks in end of main section,
sew curlicue ends to main section.
With RS facing, rejoin yarn to top of
3ch at beg of last row of curlicue
end. 1ch, 1sc into first st, [14ch, 4dc
into 4th ch from hook, 4dc into each
ch, ss into last sc] (curlicue made),
1sc into next 2sts of curlicue end,
work 1 curlicue as before, 1sc into
next 3 sts; rep from * to start of main
section omitting last rep, ending
1 curlicue in last st.
Fasten off.
Work along opposite edge of
curlicue end to match. With RS
facing, join yarn to right corner at
other end of main section, make
31ch, then complete as other end.

MAKING UP
Press under a damp cloth on the
main section only, leaving the
curlique ends unpressed.

*Twisted curlicues and masses of
bobbles create lots of texture*

Materials
2 x 100g balls of Knitglobal Nazca Baby
Alpaca, white (A)
2 x 100g balls of Knitglobal Nazca Baby
Alpaca, black (B)
G/6 (4.50 mm) crochet hook

Size
60 x 14½ in. (152 x 37 cm).

Gauge
24 st to 6 in. (15 cm) and 4 rows to 2¾ in.
(7 cm) over patt, with G/6 (4.50 mm)
hook.

Abbreviations
ch chain
cont continue
dc double crochet
patt pattern
rep repeat
ss slip stitch
st(s) stitch(es)
tch turning chain

domino alpaca shawl

This classic black and white shawl will never date and was inspired by a set of dominos scattered across the carpet. I liked the strong contrast of the black dots on the white background, so I tried to achieve the same effect in this dramatic shawl. It is made in in the most wonderful super-soft baby Alpaca yarn.

SHAWL

Using A, make 246ch.
Row 1: With A, 1dc into 4th ch from hook, 1dc into each ch to end, turn. (244 sts)
Row 2: With B, 3ch, (count as 1dc), skip first dc, 1dc into each of next 5dc, 8ch, skip 8dc, *1dc into each of next 4dc, 8ch, skip 8dc; rep from * to last 2 sts, 1dc into last dc, 1dc into top of tch, turn.
Row 3: With B, 8ch, skip first 2dc and 4ch, 1dc into each of next 4ch, *8ch, skip next 4dc and 4ch, 1dc into each of next 4ch; rep from * to last 6 sts, 4ch, skip 4dc, 1dc into next dc, 1dc into top of tch, turn.
Row 4: With B, 3ch, (count as 1dc), skip first dc, 1dc into next dc, *1dc into each of next 4ch, 8ch, skip 4dc and 4ch; rep from * ending 1dc into eachof next 2ch, turn.
Cont in stripes of 4 rows A and 4 rows B.
Row 5: 3ch, (count as 1dc), skip first dc, 1dc into each dc and ch to end, 1dc into top of tch, turn. (244 sts)

Row 6: 3ch, (count as 1dc), skip first dc, 1dc into next dc, *8ch, skip 8dc, 1dc into each of next 4dc; rep from * to last 2 sts, 1ch, 1dc into next dc, 1dc into top of tch, turn.
Row 7: 3ch, (count as 1dc), skip first dc, 1dc into next dc, *8ch, skip next 4dc and 4ch, 1dc into each of next 4ch; rep from * to last 2 sts, 1dc into next dc, 1dc into top of tch, turn.
Row 8: 3ch, (count as 1dc), skip first dc, 1dc into next dc, *8ch, skip next 4dc and 4ch, 1dc into each of next 4ch; rep from * to last 2 sts, 1dc into next dc, 1dc into top of tch, turn.
Row 9: 3ch, (count as 1dc), skip first dc, 1dc into each dc and ch to end, turn. (244 dc)
Rep Rows 2–9 once, then Rows 2–5 once again.
Fasten off.

MAKING UP

Chain stitch round a few selected holes with opposite color, as shown in photo. Leave ends after tying off.

Classic black and white will never date

sparkle arm warmers

The pretty ruffles at the cuffs of these seductive sparkly arm warmers add a touch of drama and femininity. Wear them with anything from evening dress to jeans—you'll never look out of place!

Materials
2 x 50g balls of Bouton d'or, color 399 (A)
2 x 50g balls of Lantarus Queen, color 071 (B)
F/5 (4.00 mm) crochet hook

Size
Upper arm width 11½ in. (29 cm); length to wrist 15 in. (38 cm), excluding ruffle.

Gauge
5 patt repeats to 3½ in. (9 cm) × 26 rows to 4 in. (10 cm) over patt, using F/5 (4.00 mm) hook.

Abbreviations
ch chain
ch sp chain space
dec decrease
patt pattern
rep repeat
RS right side
sc single crochet
ss slip stitch
st(s) stitch(es)
WS wrong side

GLOVES
(Make 2)
With A, make 64ch.

Row 1: 1sc into 4th ch from hook, *3ch, 1sc into next ch, 3ch, skip 2ch, 1sc into next ch; rep from * to end, turn. (15 patts)

Row 2: 3ch, *[1sc, 3ch, 1sc] into next 3ch sp, 3ch, skip next 3ch sp; rep from * ending with 1sc into last 3ch, turn.

Rep Row 2 twice more.

Taking dec into the pattern, work as follows:

Row 5 (dec row): Ss into first 3ch sp, 1ch, [1sc, 3ch, 1sc] into same 3ch sp, *3ch, skip next 3ch sp, [1sc, 3ch, 1sc] into next 3ch sp; rep from * ending with 3ch, 1sc into last 3ch, turn.

Row 6: Ss into first 3ch sp, 1ch, [1sc, 3ch, 1sc] into first 3ch sp, *3ch, skip next 3ch sp, [1sc, 3ch, 1sc] into next 3ch sp; rep from * to last 3ch sp, 3ch, 1sc into last sc, turn.

Rows 7–10: 1ch, [1sc, 3ch, 1sc] into first 3ch sp, *3ch, skip next 3ch sp, [1sc, 3ch, 1sc] into next 3ch sp; rep from * to last 3ch sp, 3ch, 1sc into last sc, turn.

Row 11 (dec row): 1ch, 1sc into first 3ch sp, *3ch, skip next 3ch sp, [1sc, 3ch, 1sc] into next 3ch sp; rep from * to last 3ch sp, 2ch, 1sc into last sc, turn.

Rows 12–16: 1ch, 1sc into first 2ch sp, *3ch, skip next 3ch sp, [1sc, 3ch, 1sc] into next 3ch sp; rep from * ending 1sc into last sc, turn.

Row 17 (dec row): Ss into 2nd sc, 1ch, 1sc into this sc, 2ch, skip next 3ch sp, *[1sc, 3ch, 1sc] into next 3ch sp, 3ch, skip next 3ch sp]; rep from * to last 3ch sp, [1sc, 3ch, 1sc] into this sp, 1ch, 1sc into last sc, turn.

Rows 18–22: 1ch, 1sc into first sc, 2ch, skip next 3ch sp, *[1sc, 3ch, 1sc] into next 3ch sp, 3ch, skip next 3ch sp; rep from * ending with [1sc, 3ch, 1sc] intonext 3ch sp, 2ch, skip last 3ch sp, 1sc into last sc, turn.

Row 23 (dec row): 3ch, skip first 3ch sp, *[1sc, 3ch, 1sc] into next 3ch sp, 3ch, skip 3ch sp; rep from * to last 2ch sp, working 1sc into last sc, turn.

Rows 24–28: 3ch, *[1sc, 3ch, 1sc] into next 3ch sp, 3ch, skip next 3ch sp; rep from * ending 1sc into last 3ch sp, turn.

Rep Rows 5 to 28 inclusive once more, then work straight as Row 2, until work measures 15 in. (38 cm).
Cuff
Fasten off A, join in B.
Row 1: 3ch, *[1sc, 3ch, 1sc] into next 3ch sp, 3ch, 1sc into next 3ch sp, 3ch; rep from * to last 3ch sp, [1sc, 3ch, 1sc] into this sp, turn.
Row 2: 3ch, 1sc into first 3ch sp, *[3ch, (1sc, 3ch, 1sc) into next 3ch sp] twice, 3ch, 1sc into 3ch sp; rep from * to last 3ch sp, 3ch, [1sc, 3ch, 1sc] into this sp, turn.
Row 3: 3ch, 1sc into first 3ch sp, *[3ch, (1sc, 3ch, 1sc)] into next 3ch sp; rep from * to end, turn.
Row 4: 3ch, *[1sc, 3ch, 1sc] into 3ch sp, 3ch, skip next 3ch sp; rep from * ending 1sc into last 3ch sp, turn.
Rep Rows 3 and 4 once more.
Row 7: 3ch, [1sc, 3ch, 1sc] into first 3ch sp, *3ch, skip next 3ch sp, [1sc, 3ch, 1sc] into next 3ch sp; rep from * to end.
Row 8: 3ch, skip first 3ch sp, *[1sc, 3ch, 1sc] into next 3ch sp, 3ch, skip next 3ch sp; rep from * ending 1sc into last 3ch sp.
Fasten off.

MAKING UP
With WS facing, join seam.

summer days hat

Ice cream, candyfloss, seaside ponies, clapboard pastel-painted beach huts... and a floppy hat that will keep you cool under the hot sun, shade your eyes, make you feel good. This is certainly the one, crocheted in beautiful soft linen drape. Make several in a variety of pastel colors to go with all your summer outfits.

Materials
1 x 50g ball of Rowan Linen Drape, color 861 (A)
1 x 50g ball of Rowan Linen Drape, color 844 (B)
1 x 50g ball of Rowan Linen Drape, color 845 (C)
C/2 (2.75 mm) crochet hook
E/4 (3.50 mm) crochet hook

Size
One size, to fit average adult head.

Gauge
11 sc x 12 rows to 2 in. (5 cm) over sc using C/2 (2.75 mm) hook.

Abbreviations
ch chain
rep repeat
sc single crochet
ss slip stitch
st(s) stitch(es)
yoh yarn over hook

Special abbreviations
Reverse sc (crab stitch) = sc worked from left to right. Insert hook into the next st to the right, yoh, pull the yarn through, twisting hook to face upwards at the same time, yoh and draw through to finish off the sc as normal. Working in this direction causes a twist that gives a decorative edge.

Notes

Work the following color sequence throughout: A × 4 rounds; B × 2 rounds; C × 4 rounds.
Break off yarn after each band of color and weave into stitches.
The hat is worked as one piece.

HAT

Using C/2 (2.75 mm) hook and A, make 2ch.

Round 1 (RS): 10sc into 2nd ch, ss into first sc, turn. (10 sc)

Round 2: 1ch, 2sc into each sc, ss into first sc, turn. (20 sc)

Round 3: 1ch, [2sc into next sc, 1sc into next sc] to end, ss into first sc, turn. (30 sc)

Round 4: 1ch, 1sc into each sc, ss into first sc, turn.

Round 5: As Round 3. (45 sc)

Round 6: As Round 4.

Round 7: 1ch, [2sc into next sc, 1 sc into next 2sc] to end, ss into first sc, turn. (60 sc)

Rounds 8–9: As Round 4.

Round 10: 1ch, [2sc into next st, 1sc into 3sc] to end, ss into first sc, turn. (75 sc)

Round 11: As Round 4.

Round 12: 1ch, [2sc into next sc, 1sc into next 4sc] to end, ss into first sc, turn. (90 sc)

Rounds 13–16: As Round 4.

Round 17: 1ch, [2sc into next sc, 1sc into next 5sc] to end, ss into first sc, turn. (105 sc)

Rounds 18–23: As Round 4.

Round 24: 1ch, [2sc into next sc, 1sc into next 20sc] to end, ss into first sc, turn. (110 sc)

Rounds 25–34: As Round 4.

Change to E/4 (3.50 mm) hook.

Rounds 35–39: As Round 4.

Round 40: 1ch, [2sc into next sc, 1sc into next 10sc] to end, ss into first sc, turn. (120 sc)

Rounds 41–42: As Round 4.

Round 43: 1ch, [2sc into next sc, 1sc into next 4sc] to end, ss into first sc, turn. (144 sc)

Rounds 44–48: As Round 4.

Round 49: 1ch, [2sc into next sc, 1sc into next 12sc] to end, ss into first sc, turn. (156 sc)

Rounds 50–52: As Round 4.

Work edging

With RS facing and using C/2 (2.75 mm) hook and B, work 1 round of reverse sc into last round, ss into first sc.

Fasten off.

A floppy linen summer hat in pretty pastel colors, just perfect for lazy days in the sun

Materials
3 x 50g balls of Sirdar Organza, color 287
G/6 (4.50 mm) crochet hook

Size
One size, to fit average adult head.

Gauge
10 sts x 10 rows to 4 in. (10 cm) with G/6
(4.50 mm) hook.

Abbreviations
ch chain
sc single crochet
rdc raised double crochet
ss slip stitch
st(s) stitch(es)
dc double

Note
The twists on the last round can be
graduated in size to appear longer at the
back or the sides—for each slight variation
just add 1ch to initial ch length of 5.

silky cloche hat

Dancing at teatime and early evening wearing beautiful silky
hats—the "Bloomsbury set" enjoyed life to the full. This
evening-style cloche is reminiscent of Bloomsbury style and
the decorative edging mimics the tight curls peeping from
under ladies' hats. The shaping swirls round the head,
achieved by increasing at a certain point in the design.

Hat
Wrap the yarn round two fingers to
form a ring.
Round 1: 8sc in ring, pull ring tight,
ss to first sc.
Round 2: 1ch, 2sc into each sc, ss
into first sc. (16 sc)
Round 3: 1ch, [2sc in next sc, 1rdc
round stem of next sc] 8 times, ss
into first sc. (24 sts)
Round 4: 1ch, [1sc into each of 2sc,
1sc into rdc, 1rdc round stem of rdc
in round below] 8 times, ss into first
sc. (32 sts)
Round 5: 1ch, [1sc into each of 3sc,
1sc into rdc, 1rdc round stem of rdc
in round below] 8 times, ss into first
sc. (40 sts)
Round 6: 1ch, [1sc into each of 4sc,
1sc into rdc, 1rdc round stem of rdc
in round below] 8 times, ss into first
sc. (48 sts)

Round 7: 1ch, [1sc into each of 5sc,
1sc into rdc, 1rdc round stem of rdc
in round below] 8 times, ss into first
sc. (56 sts)
Round 8: 1ch, [skip 1sc into each of
5sc, 1sc in rdc, 1rdc round stem of
rdc in round below] 8 times, ss into
first sc. (56 sts)
Rounds 9–19: as Round 8.
Round 20: 3ch, [1dc into each sc to
rdc, 1dc into rdc, 5ch, skip first ch,
3sc into each ch, ss into top of last
dc] 8 times, ss into top of 3ch.
Fasten off.
Do not block.

*The decorative edging mirrors
the tight curls peeping from
under ladies' hats*

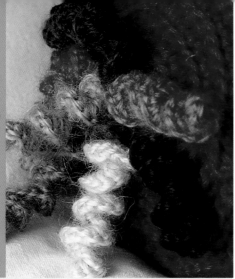

Materials
1 x 100g ball of Wensleydale DK, pomegranate
Oddments of Wensleydale DK in eight different colors for corkscrew curls
E/4 (3.50 mm) crochet hook
I/9 (5.50 mm) crochet hook

Size
One size, to fit average adult head.

Gauge
14 st x 22 rows to 2 in. (5 cm) over sc worked into back loops on I/9 (5.50 mm) hook.

Abbreviations
ch chain
sc single crochet
foll following
rep repeat
ss slip stitch
st(s) stitch(es)

Special abbreviations
sc2tog—single crochet two together, insert hook into next st, wrap yarn over hook, draw a loop through; rep this step into the next st (3 loops on the hook), wrap yarn and draw through all loops on the hook to complete.

twizzle hat

The explosive cluster of twists at the crown of this hat and the riotous circus colors all demand attention! The inspiration for this design was the marvelous richness and clarity of the colors available in the yarn. You only need a tiny amount for each twist, so this is an ideal way to use up some of those left-over scraps.

HAT
Use yarn double throughout. Work in back loop only of each st.
Using I/9 (5.50 mm) hook, make 2ch.
Round 1: 12sc in first ch, ss in first sc, 1ch, turn. (12 sc)
Round 2: 2sc in each st, ss in first sc, 1ch, turn. (24 sc)
Round 3: 1sc in each st, ss in first sc, 1ch, turn. (24 sc)
Round 4: *2sc in next st, 1sc in foll st; rep from *, ss in first sc, 1ch, turn. (36 sc)
Round 5: 1sc in each st, ss in first sc, 1ch, turn. (36 sc)
Round 6: *2sc in next st, 1sc in each of foll 2 sts; rep from *, ss in first sc, 1ch, turn. (48 sc)
Round 7: 1sc in each st, ss in first sc, 1ch, turn. (48 sc)
Round 8: *2sc in next st, 1sc in each of foll 3 sts; rep from *, ss in first sc, 1ch, turn. (60 sc)
Round 9: 1sc in each st, ss in first sc, 1ch, turn. (60 sc)
Round 10: *2sc in next st, 1sc in each of foll 4 sts; rep from *, ss in first sc, 1ch, turn. (72 sc)
Round 11: 1sc in each st, ss in first sc, 1ch, turn. (72 sc)
Round 12: *2sc in next st, 1sc in each of foll 5 sts; rep from *, ss in first sc, 1ch, turn. (84 sc)
Round 13: 1sc in each st, ss in first sc, 1ch, turn. (84 sc)

Round 14: *2sc in first st, 1sc in each of foll 6 sts; rep from *, ss in first sc, 1ch, turn. (96 sc)
Rounds 15–20: 1sc in each st, ss in first sc, 1ch, turn. (96 sc)
Round 21: *Sc2tog, 1sc in each of next 6 sts; rep from *, ss in first sc, 1ch, turn. (84 sc)
Round 22: *Sc2tog, 1sc in each of next 5 sts; rep from *, ss in first sc, 1ch, turn. (72 sc)
Rounds 23–31: 1sc in each st, ss in first sc, 1ch, turn. (72 sc)
Ribbing edge
Change to E/4 (3.50 mm) hook. Work ribbing in rows.
Row 2: Working in back loop only, 1sc in each of next 4sts, 1ch, turn.
Row 3: Working in back loop only, 1sc in each of next 4 sts, ss in each of next 2sts of last round of hat.
Rep Rows 2–3 round last row of hat. At end of last row of ribbing, working through back loop and opp side of foundation ch, ss in each of next 4 sts.

CORKSCREW CURLS
(make one in each shade)
Using E/4 (3.50 mm) hook and yarn double, make 14ch, skip first ch, 4dc in each ch. Fasten off leaving a 4 in. (10 cm) end. Sew to center top of hat.

Materials

2 x 50g balls of Rowan Tapestry, color 157, moorland
P/16 (12.00 mm) crochet hook
G/6 (4.00 mm) crochet hook
Safety pin or contrast yarn for marker

Size

One size, to fit average adult head.

Gauge

8½sts to 4 in. (10 cm) over dc, with P/16 (12.00 mm) hook and using yarn double (before fulling).

Abbreviations

ch chain
cont continue
dc double crochet
rep repeat
sc single crochet
sp(s) space(s)
ss slip stitch
st(s) stitch(es)

Special abbreviations

dc2tog—double 2 together, leaving last loop of each st on hook, work 1dc into each of next 2dc, yarn over hook and draw through all three loops.

cashmere helmet

The way the light interplayed with the fiber of this beautiful yarn, creating highlights and shadows, inspired the design. The hat is fulled by hand so the colors mingle and blend like a distant hillside clothed in claret, greens and pale blue.

HELMET

Using yarn double and P/16 (12.00 mm) hook, 3ch, ss into first ch to form a ring.

Round 1: 3ch, 11dc into ring, ss into top of 3ch. (12 sts)
Round 2: 3ch, 1dc into same place as ss, 2dc into each dc, ss into top of 3ch. (24 sts)
Round 3: 3ch, 1dc into same place as ss, [1dc into next dc, 2dc into next dc] 11 times, 1dc into last dc, ss into top of 3ch. (36 sts)
Round 4: 3ch, 1dc into same place as ss, [1dc into each of next 2dc, 2dc into next dc] 11 times, 1dc into each of last 2dc, ss into top of 3ch. (48 sts)
Round 5: 3ch, 1dc into same place as ss, [1dc into each of next 11dc, 2dc into next dc] 3 times, 1dc into each of last 11dc, ss into top of 3ch. (52 sts)
Cont, working into sps between dc.
Rounds 6–14: Ss into sp before first dc, 3ch, 1dc into each sp, ss into top of 3ch.

Right ear flap

First row: Ss into sp before first dc, 3ch, 2dc into next sp, 1dc into each of next 7sps, 2dc into next sp, turn. (12 sts)
Work 3 rows.
Work dc2tog at each end of next row. (10 sts)
Work 2 rows.

Fasten off.
Skip 19 sps after right ear flap for forehead, rejoin yarn to next sp and work left ear flap to match right ear flap.

Ruffle

Using one strand of yarn and G/6 (4.00 mm) hook, make a 4¾ in. (12 cm) length of ch.
Row 1: Skip 3ch, 3dc into single strand of each ch, turn.
Row 2: 3sc into each st.

EDGING

Using one strand of yarn and G/6 (4.00 mm) hook attach yarn at center back neck, [1sc into st, 3ch, 1sc into each of next 2 sts] all round edge, ss into first sc.
Fasten off.

MAKING UP

Allow ruffle to curl up unevenly, press and stitch onto side of helmet. Wash by hand in warmer than normal water and rub hard to full the hat—not felt it.

bejeweled shrug

The colors of the seasons often play an important role in my designs. This shrug uses wonderful, warm fall hues inspired by the changing shades of the leaves with beads to represent the glistening early morning dew.

Materials

1 x 50g ball of Trendsetter Yarns Mohair, marmalade
11375 stitch'n'craft beads, mix of orange with lime lining and black
C/2 (3.00 mm) crochet hook
No. 12 steel (0.75 mm) crochet hook

Size

Length 11½ in. (28 cm) excluding edging; width 48 in. (120 cm).

Gauge

32dc to 4 in. (10 cm) using C/2 (3.00 mm) crochet hook.

Abbreviations

beg beginning
ch chain
ch sp chain space
dc double crochet
hdc half double
RS right side
sc single crochet
WS wrong side

SHRUG

Using C/2 (3.00 mm) hook, make 90ch.

Row 1: Place marker at beg of row, 1dc into 4th ch from hook, [1dc into each ch] to end. (90 sts)
Work 9 rows dc.
Start arched mesh.

Row 11: 6ch, 1sc in 10th ch from hook, *5ch, skip 3ch, 1sc in next ch; rep from * to end, turn.

Row 12: 6ch, *1sc in next ch sp, 5ch; rep from * ending 1sc in last ch sp, 2ch, 1dc in 4th of 9ch, turn.

Row 13: 6ch, 1sc in first 5ch sp, *5ch, 1sc in next ch sp; rep from * to end, turn.

Row 14: As Row 12, ending 1dc in first of 6ch, turn. Start large mesh.

Row 15: 1dc in 6th ch from hook, *1ch, skip 1ch, 1dc in next ch; rep from * to end, turn.

Row 16: 4ch, skip first dc and 1ch, *1dc in next dc, 1ch, skip 1ch; rep from * ending 1dc in next ch, turn.

Rows 17–18: As Rows 15–16.

Row 19: 1dc in 8th ch from hook, *2ch, skip 2ch, 1dc in next ch; rep from * to end, turn.

Rows 20: 5ch, skip first dc and 2ch, *1dc in next dc, 2ch, skip 2ch; rep from * ending 1dc in next ch, turn.

Row 21: 1dc in 8th ch from hook, *2ch, skip 2ch, 1dc in next ch; rep from * to end, turn. Start decreasing.

Row 22: *1dc in next dc, skip 2ch, 1dc; rep from * to end.
Rep Row 22 six more times. 30ch.

CENTER PANEL

Break yarn, rejoin to first of 90ch with RS facing to work in opp direction. Start arched mesh.

Row 1: 6ch, 1sc in 10th ch from hook, *5ch, skip 3ch, 1sc in next ch; rep from * to end, turn.

Row 2: 6ch, *1sc in next ch sp, 5ch; rep from* ending 1sc in last ch sp, 2ch, 1dc in 4th of 9ch, turn.

Row 3: 6ch, 1sc in first 5ch sp, *5ch, 1sc in next ch sp; rep from * to end, turn.

Row 4: As Row 2 ending 1dc in first of 6ch, turn.

Row 5–8: As Rows 1–4.
Start large mesh.

Row 9: 1dc in 6th ch from hook, *1ch, skip 1ch, 1dc in next ch; rep from * to end, turn.

Row 10: 4ch, skip first dc and 1ch, *1dc in next dc, 1ch, skip 1ch; rep from * ending 1dc in next ch, turn.
Rep Rows 9–10 six more times.

Rows 38–39: Work 30hdc.
Break yarn, thread approx 200 beads.

Rows 40–43: Work 4 rows hdc with beaded yarn.

Rows 44–45: Work 30hdc.
Start large mesh.

Row 46–49: As Rows 9–10.
Start arched mesh.

Row 70–73: As Rows 1–4.

Rows 74–77: As Rows 1–4.
Cont in double mesh on 90 sts.

Row 78: 1dc in 8th ch from hook, *2ch, skip 2ch, 1dc in next ch; rep from * to end, turn.

Row 79: 5ch, skip first dc and 2ch, *1dc in next dc, 2ch, skip 2ch; rep from * ending 1dc in next ch, turn.

Row 80: As Row 78.
Start decreasing.

Row 81: *1dc in next dc, skip 2ch, 1dc; rep from * to end.
Rep Row 81 six more times. (30 ch)

NECK RUFFLE

Row 1: 1 dc in every ch between 2 markers.

Next row: 2dc in every dc.

Next row: 4dc in every dc.

Bead edges

Either thread beads on yarn for final row and pull up as required, or thread yarn after finishing last row and catch the beads along edges of neck ruffle and wrist ruffle.

ROSES

(make 4)

Make 35ch. 1dc in each ch, gather up and stitch down.

MAKING UP

Using slip stitch, fasten roses on each sleeve between wrist and underarm.

hydrangea blues scarf

The beautiful shades of blue in a bowl of fading hydrangea heads inspired this design—and because the weather was turning colder it seemed appropriate to make a scarf. The pompoms reminded me of the shape of the rounded flower heads. Using the super large needle combined with the crochet hook was great fun.

Materials

2 x 50g balls of Rowan RY Classic Baby Alpaca, color 202, thistle (A)
2 x 50g balls of Rowan RY Classic Silk Wool, color 305, clay (B)
H/8 (5.00 mm) crochet hook
US 50 (25 mm) knitting needle
Pompom maker
Organza and satin ribbon to tone with yarn
Seed beads and large, light-weight bead
Fine sewing needle
Thread to match ribbon

Size

Length 38 in. (96 cm) including pompoms

Gauge

20 sts to 4 in. (10 cm) and 9 rows to 4³/₄ in. (12 cm) over patt using H/8 (5.00 mm) hook.

Abbreviations

ch chain
sc single crochet
ss slip stitch
yoh yarn over hook

PATTERN

Use 1 strand of A and 1 strand of B together throughout. Make 28ch.

Row 1: Sl loop onto knitting needle and remove hook, tighten yarn. Balance blunt end of needle on your lap with point facing upwards, skip first ch, [insert hook in next ch and draw loop through, sl loop onto needle and remove hook, tighten yarn to keep gauge even] 27 times, turn. (28 loops on needle)

Row 2: Insert hook through first 4 loops and drop them off needle, yoh and draw loop through, yoh and draw through loop, work 4sc into this set of loops, [insert hook through next 4 loops and drop them off needle, work 4sc into this set of loops] 6 imes, turn. (28 sc)

Row 3: Working into back loops only work 1ss in each sc, turn.

Row 4: Sl loop onto needle and remove hook, tighten yarn, skip first ss, [insert hook into back loop of next ss and draw loop through, sl loop onto needle and remove hook, tighten yarn to keep gauge even] 27 times, turn. (28 loops on needle)

Rep Rows 2–4 until scarf measures 36¹/₂ in. (91 cm) from beginning, ending with a Row 4.

Next row: As Row 2 but work 2sc not 4 into each group of 4 loops. (14 sc)

Next row: As Row 3.

Next row: As Row 4 but work into 2nd ss then every alt ss to end. (8 loops on needle)

Next row: As Row 2 but work 2sc not 4 into each group of 4 loops. (4 sc)

Next row: As Row 3.

Fasten off.

POMPOMS

Make 6 pompoms in varying sizes, colors and yarn mixtures. Make chains of varying lengths to attach pompoms to straight end of scarf. Work one large pompom, including lengths of organza and satin ribbon with your yarn as you wrap it round the pompom maker. Using a fine needle and matching thread, stitch clusters of seed beads to the ends of the organza ribbon in the large pompom. Make a short length of ch and attach to shaped end of scarf. Thread a large bead then join on pompom.

attitude gloves

Lacy gloves with attitude—these stylish accessories will add drama and character to even the simplest outfit. The gold gloves shown here have cropped fingers with a row of glass beads set round the finger ends. The variation shown on page 41 is made in two shades of aqua, with full length fingers.

Materials
1 × 50g ball of Presencia Finca Perle cotton No 8, gold
1 × 50g ball of Presencia Finca Perle cotton No 8, aqua
1 × 50g ball of Presencia Finca Perle cotton No 8, dark aqua
No. 8 steel (1.50 mm) crochet hook
Beads

Size
One size, to fit average adult hand.

Gauge
The mesh stretches, so it is difficult to give a precise gauge.

Abbreviations
beg beginning
ch chain
ch sp chain space
dec decrease
foll following
inc increase
patt pattern
rep repeat
RS right side
sc single crochet
ss slip stitch
st(s) stitch(es)

GLOVES
(Make 2)
Starting at the wrist, make 80ch, ss into first ch to make a ring.
Round 1: 5ch, skip 3ch, 1sc in next ch, [5ch, skip 3ch, 1sc in next ch] 20 times, ss into top of first 5ch arch at beg of round.
Round 2: 5ch, 1sc in next 5ch arch, [5ch, 1sc into next 5ch arch] 20 times, ss into top of first 5ch arch at beg of round.
Rep Round 2 until there are 20 rounds of ch arch.
Round 23: 30ch, skip 4ch arch, 1sc in next ch arch (this forms the opening for the thumb), work a row of ch arch, 5ch, skip 2sts of ch, sc in next st.
Round 24: *5ch, skip 4ch, 1sc in next st, rep from * 4 times, patt to end.

Round 25: 5ch, 1sc in next ch arch (there should be 21 ch arch in this row).
Rounds 26–33: Work 8 more rows as Row 2 and cont loops to left of thumb opening.
Fingers for full glove
Fold work with thumb opening at extreme left and work first finger directly over thumb.
Work 5ch arch over back of glove, 5ch, 1sc in 4th of 5ch arch on inside front of glove making 6 free 5ch arch for finger, work six 5ch arch, 5ch, 1sc in center st of ch between fingers, 5ch, 1sc in next free 5ch arch. (5ch arch)
Cont working in patt in 5ch arch until there are 8 rounds for little finger and 10 rounds for a long finger, then work 4 rounds of 4ch arch, 2 rounds of 2ch arch, 2ch, 1sc in each 5ch arch, draw sts tog to close finger tip, fasten off.
Middle finger
Join thread to bottom of forefinger on back of glove, work three 5ch arch, 5ch, sc in 2nd of 5ch arch on inside of glove, work 1ch arch, 5ch, sc in first loop between fingers, 5ch, sc in loop between fingers, 5ch, sc in center st of ch arch between fingers, 5ch, sc in next free ch. (7ch arch)
Cont work until there are 10 rows.

Lacy gloves with attitude will add drama and character to any outfit

Tips

● As you work the mesh design for these gloves you will be amazed to find that it has a slight elasticity, which is just perfect for these gloves. This is due to the yarn, so it will not be the same if you choose an alternative yarn to make the project.

● When choosing beads for use in knitting and crochet projects, buy from a reputable supplier. A size 6 is usually fine for crochet cotton—just make sure that the central hole is large enough so the yarn you are using will pass through easily. Glass beads are better than plastic, which may melt at high temperatures or if caught with an iron.

● Handwash these gloves as needed and dry flat.

● There are so many colors available in the Presencia yarn that you will be spoilt for choice!

Work 6 rows of 4ch arch, 3 rows of 2ch arch and finish same as forefinger.

Ring finger
Work first 10 rows same as middle finger and then finish same as forefinger.

Little finger
Work 8 rows of 5ch arch and finish same as forefinger.

Thumb
Join thread to lower right side of opening and work twelve 5ch arch, work 3 more rows of 12 ch arch each.

Next row: Work three 5ch arch, sc in next loop omitting the ch between; rep from beg twice (dec 3 ch arch), work one row of ch arch.

Next row: Dec 2 ch arch on inside of thumb and work 1 more row of 5ch arch then work 4 rows of 8ch arch, 1sc in each ch arch and finish off same as fingers.

Fingers for cropped gloves
Work all fingers as for full glove, but length is determined by reaching first joint of middle finger.

Last row: 3ch, 1sc in next ch arch. Fasten off.

CUFFS

Thread beads onto yarn if desired and stitch round top edge of all fingers and thumb.

Full gloves

Change to a contrast color and thread red beads onto yarn.

Rows 1–3: 5ch, sc in next 5ch arch. Change back to main color.

Rows 4–5: 5ch, sc in next 5ch arch, placing beads as shown.

Fasten off.

Cropped gloves

Row 1: 5ch, 1sc in every other 5ch arch.

Row 2: 5ch, sc in every 5ch arch.

Fasten off.

Variations

The variation on this pattern above has completed fingers and also uses two different colors of yarn—the darker color at the base accentuates the shape of the cuff a little more.

The beads round the ends of the cropped fingers must be omitted here, so for extra sparkle, you could work beads along the edge of the cuff instead—or even stitch sequins on after the gloves are finished.

Materials
3 x 50g balls of Twilleys Spirit, fire
F/5 (4.00 mm) crochet hook

Size
One size, to fit average adult head.

Gauge
18 sts x 17 rows to 4 in. (10 cm) over
pattern using F/5 (4.00 mm) hook.

Abbreviations
ch chain
sc single crochet
dec decrease
hdc half double
inc increase
patt pattern
rep repeat
rem remain
RS right side
sp(s) space(s)
ss slip stitch
st(s) stitch(es)
tch turning chain
dc double
WS wrong side

Special abbreviations
sc2tog—single crochet two together;
insert hook into next st, wrap yarn over
hook, draw a loop through; rep this step
into the next st (3 loops on the hook),
wrap yarn and draw through all loops on
the hook to complete.
sc3tog—single crochet three together;
insert hook into next st, wrap yarn over
hook, draw a loop through; rep this step
into the next st twice (3 loops on the
hook), wrap yarn and draw through all
loops on the hook to complete.

squared beret

Memories of a misty, murky Scottish morning in October led
to this design. I first created it in knitting, then translated the
pattern into crochet instead. After completing the crochet the
corners are pulled together and stitched to the edging band to
give the beret its billowing shape. The flower trim is made
separately and stitched onto the band as a finishing touch.

BERET
Make 27 ch.
Row 1: Skip 3ch (count as 1dc), [1sc
into next ch, 1dc into next ch] to
end, turn. (25 sts)
Row 2: 3ch (counts as 1dc), skip first
dc, [1sc into next sc, 1dc into next
dc] to end working last dc into top
of 3ch, turn.
Row 3 (inc row): 1ch, [1sc, 1dc]
into first dc, [1sc into next sc, 1dc
into next dc] to end, ending 1sc into
last sc, [1dc, 1sc] into top of 3ch,
turn. (1 st inc at each end)
Row 4 (inc row): 3ch, 1sc into first
sc, [1dc into next dc, 1sc into next
sc] to end, ending 1dc into last dc,
[1sc, 1dc] into last sc, turn. (1 st inc
at each end)
Rep Rows 3–4 until there are 73 sts.
Place marker at each end of last row.
Now work straight, rep Row 2, until
work measures 11½ in. (29 cm).
Place marker at each end of last row.
Next row: Ss into first dc and first sc,
1ch, 1sc into same sc, [1dc into next
dc, 1sc into next sc] to within tch,
turn. (1 st dec at each end)
Next row: Ss into first sc and first dc,
2ch, (count as first st), [1sc into next
sc, 1dc into next dc] to last 2 sts,
1hdc in last dc, turn. (1 st dec at
each end)

Rep these last 2 rows until 25 sts
rem.
Work 2 rows straight, working last
dc into top of 2ch on first row.
Fasten off.

BORDER
Starting at the center of the lower
straight edge (the 27ch at the start),
work 1ch, 1sc into each base ch to
start of diagonal shaping, ignore this
shaping, work 25sc evenly along next
straight edge (between markers),
ignore next diagonal shaping, 1sc
into each 25 sts along next top
straight edge, ignore next diagonal
shaping, work 25sc evenly along next
straight edge (between markers),
ignore next diagonal shaping, work
1sc into each of rem base ch, ss into
first sc, turn. (100 sc)
Next round: 1ch, 1sc into same place
as ss, 1sc into each sc, working
sc3tog into 3 sts at each corner, ss
into first sc, turn. (92 sts)
Next round: 1ch, work in sc, at same
time dec 2 sts evenly spaced along
each of the four sides, working each
dec as sc2tog, ss into first sc, turn.
(84 sts)
Next round: 1ch, 1sc into each st, ss
into first sc, turn.

Rep last round until border measures 3 in. (7.5 cm), ending with a WS row.

Picot edging

With RS facing, work 1ch, [1sc, 3ch, 1sc] into first st, *skip next st, [1sc, 3ch, 1sc] into next st; rep from * to last st, 1sc into last st, ss into first sc. Fasten off.

FLOWER

Make 2ch.

Round 1: 20dc into first ch, ss into first dc to form a circle.

Round 2: Working into front loop only, 1ch, 1sc into same place as ss, 3ch, ss into top of sc, (picot made), *1sc into each of next 2dc, 3ch, ss into top of last sc, (picot made); rep from * ending 1sc into last dc, ss into first sc.

Round 3: Working into back loop only, ss into first back loop, 1ch, 1sc into same place as ss, 5ch, skip 3dc, *1sc into next dc, 5ch, skip 3dc; rep from * ending ss into first sc.

Round 4: Ss into ch sp, [1sc, 1hdc, 3dc, 1hdc, 1sc] into each ch sp (5 petals made), ss into first sc. Fasten off.

Round 5: Rejoin yarn to back loop of center dc of a group of 3dc skipped when working Round 3, 1sc into same place as ss, *7ch, 1sc into back of center dc of next group of 3dc; rep from * to end, ss into first sc. (5 loops made)

Round 6: 1ch, [1sc, 1hdc, 2dc, 3tr, 2dc,1hdc, 1sc] into each ch sp, ss into first sc. Fasten off.

MAKING UP

With WS of beret facing, sew the four corner seams using backstitch, or crochet together using sc. Turn beret back to RS.

Sew flower onto one side of hat on the border edging.

The pleated corners of the top give this beret its stylish billowing shape

Tips

● There are many different colors available in this yarn, so choose one to suit you. Look at it in daylight against your face before buying.

● The flower trim in the same yarn adds that "certain something" to your hat. If a flower does not appeal to you, try a different design such as a curlicue or a bobble trim.

● The flower can also be made as a brooch to add to your outfit for a coordinated look. Try making the first round in black yarn—it makes the flower very eyecatching.

● When you make the trim and fasten off leave a long end, which you can use to sew the trim onto the beret securely. If you make alternative trims to match different outfits, for quick changes pin the trim to the beret with a safety pin rather than stitching in place.

jewelry

For me the process of making pieces to wear as jewelry—whether from wire, beads, felt, knitting or crochet—always starts with a memory invoked when I see a new yarn or a stone or bead. I had great fun creating these pieces, using recollections of things such as toffees for the Toffee Drop Beads, or the subtle grays of my favorite dale in Yorkshire for the Dales Gray Necker. I also used bead crochet, which is not as popular as it should be, for the Speckled Brown Bracelet and its variations.

The opportunity to buy beautiful mineral stones created over hundreds of years, and to use them with a very modern concept in yarn, has given us an unusual Mosspath Bracelet and matching brooch. Using surplus beads and crochet cotton with the simplest of stitches, I have created the Spring Flowers Necklace and Meadow Time bracelet; these pieces are ideal to pack as holiday jewelry, leaving the precious metals and precious stones at home while you have fun in the sun.

I am always inspired by the colors of the seasons, so the projects in this chapter are bright and colorful. Make your own choices—nothing needs to be exactly as shown here!

Materials
1 10g × ball of Presencia Finca Perle cotton No 8, pale pink
1 10g × ball of Presencia Finca Perle cotton No 8, dark pink
1 10g × ball of Presencia Finca Perle cotton No 8, pale green
1 10g × ball of Presencia Finca Perle cotton No 8, gold
No. 12 steel (0.75 mm) crochet hook
Size 6 pastel bead mix
Sewing needle

Size
One size.

Gauge
Gauge is not important for this project.

Abbreviations
bch bead chain
ch chain
ch sp chain space
dc double crochet
foll following
rep repeat
sc single crochet
ss slip stitch
st(s) stitch(es)

Special abbreviations
sc2tog—single crochet two stitches together; insert hook into next st, wrap yarn around hook, draw a loop through; rep this step into the next st (3 loops on the hook), wrap yarn and draw through all loops on the hook to complete.

Notes
Thread all the beads you will need onto each individual strand before commencing.

spring flowers necklace

Two-tone pink and spring-fresh green mix well—use up any spare beads that tone in this delightful necklace that matches the bracelet on page 51. Its inspiration was the same as the bracelet, but it is much softer in character and offers a great opportunity to use up all those odd accumulated beads.

DEEP PINK STRING
Using the deeper pink cotton, 8ch, work 6ch, ss to 8th ch, go back and work 1dc in each st, 9ch, 1bch, 6ch, 1bch, 24ch, 1bch, 7ch, 1bch, 3ch, 7ch 1bch, 2ch, 1bch, [4ch 1dc in each st, 2bch, 3ch] ss back on itself, 1ch, 1bch, 12ch, 1bch, 18ch, 1bch, [4ch, 2dc in each st, 2bch, 8ch, 2bch, 9ch, 2bch, 10ch, 4ch, 1bch] ss back on itself, 12ch, 1bch, 8ch, 1bch 15ch, 1bch, 4ch, 1bch, [4ch, then 1dc in each of these 4ch, 2bch, 3ch] ss back on itself, 7ch, 2bch, 5ch, 2bch, 9ch, 1bch, 8ch, 1bch, 1bch, 1ch, 1bch, 5ch 1bch, 9ch, 1bch, 6ch, 1bch. Attach to top of tab by sc across all sts and down one side. Fasten off and cut yarn leaving a 2 in. (5 cm) long end. Thread this end on a needle and feed into work to close off.

PALE PINK STRING
Work this string similar to the deep pink string but attach the two together at intervals:
Using the paler pink cotton, 12ch, 1bch, 2ch, 1bch, 8ch, 1bch, attach I green flower on 2ch, 1bch, 6ch, attach to deeper pink string with sc, 11ch, 2bch, 11ch, 1bch, 3ch, 2bch, 3ch, 1bch, 7ch, 1bch 12ch, attach to deeper pink string with sc, 8ch, 1bch, 4ch, 2bch, 3ch, ss back on

itself, 4ch, 2bch, 9ch, 2bch, 11ch, loop of 6ch, 1bch, 3ch, 1bch, 13ch, 1bch, 14ch, 1bch, 18ch, 1bch, 4ch, 2bch, 3ch, ss back on itself, attach to deeper pink string with sc, 11ch, 1bch, 5ch, 1bch, 3ch, 1bch, attach to deeper pink string with sc, 5ch, 1bch, 5ch, 1bch, 3ch, 1bch, attach to tab fastener.

GREEN STRING
Make 1 leaf: 6ch, 1dc in each of 5ch, 1sc in 6th ch, turn.
Next Row: 1sc, 5dc, 7ch, loop of 5ch, 7ch, loop 6ch, 30ch, loop 8ch, 6ch, attach 1 green flower, 8ch, 1bch, 5ch, 1bch, 6ch, 1bch, 22ch, 1bch, 3ch, 2bch, 12ch, 1bch, 3ch, 1bch, 6ch, 1bch, 6ch, make loop of 16ch, 1bch, make leaf, 11ch, 3bch, 9ch, 1bch, 5ch, 2bch, attach 1 green flower, 15ch.
Wind around the two pink strings and attach to tab fastener.

CLOSURE LOOP
Take the ends of the two pink strings and make 3 loops of 8ch each and attach together.
Tab fastener
Row 1: 3ch, 1dc in each st, 1ch. (6 sts)
Row 2: 2dc in each st. (12 sts)
Row 3: 1dc in each st. (12 sts)
Row 4: 2dc in each st. (24 sts)

Row 5: 1dc in each st. (24 sts)
Reverse shaping for next 5 rows and,
holding both sides together, change
thread to pale gold.
Row 1: Sc in each st.

Row 2: Sc2tog in every st.
Rows 3–7: Sc in each st.
Attach a bead on the end for weight.
Thread through loops for fastening.

For steps to make flower petals, see
next page.

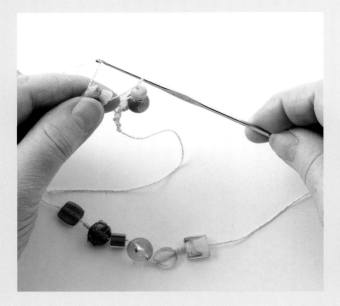

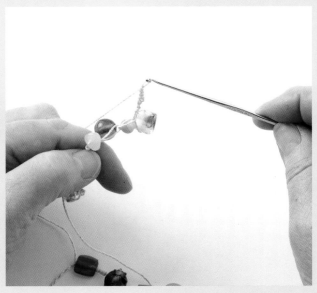

1. Make slip knot in the yarn. Make another slip knot, bringing the bead up and catching it inside the slip knot.

2. Make five chain stitches in the yarn, to create a length of chain after the bead.

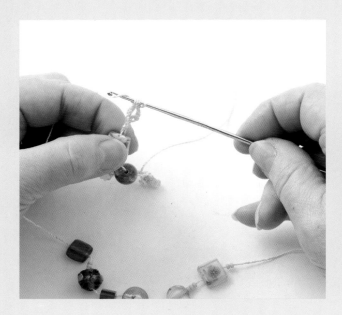

3. Return to the first chain and make a slip knot to join the chain into a ring.

4. Repeat the last three steps four times more to make five flower petals.

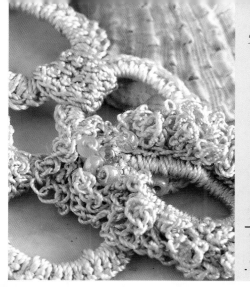

meadow time

Soft summer greens, pale and dark pink sweet peas, memories past... all went into the design of this cool-to-wear bracelet for those hot, hot summer days. The necklace on page 48 is ideal to wear with this if you make it in the same colors.

Materials

1 10g × ball of Presencia Finca Perle cotton No 8 pale pink
1 10g × ball of Presencia Finca Perle cotton No 8 dark pink
1 10g × ball of Presencia Finca Perle cotton No 8 pale green
No. 12 steel (0.75 mm) crochet hook
Size 6 pastel bead mix in pink and green

Size

$7^1/_2 \times 2^3/_4$ in. (19 × 7 cm).

Gauge

Each ring measures $1^3/_8$ in. (3.5 cm).

Abbreviations

ch chain
sc single crochet
ss slip stitch
st(s) stitch(es)

Notes

There are 3 parts to this bracelet: the circles; the tabs that hold them; and the flowers that form the fasteners.

CIRCLES

(Make 5 dark pink and 5 pale pink)
Wind a length of pink cotton around two fingers 9 times, then work 45sc into this circle, ss into first sc. Fasten off.

TABS

(Make 12 in green)
Make 13ch.

Row 1: 1sc into 2nd ch from hook, 1sc into each ch, turn.

Row 2: 1ch, 1sc into each sc to end, turn.

Row 3: As Row 2.
Fasten off.

FLOWER FASTENER

First side

Round 1: Wind the green cotton around two fingers 9 times, then work 45sc into this circle, ss into first sc.

Round 2: [10ch, skip next sc, ss into front loop of next sc] to end, ss into first ch.

Round 3: [Ss into front loop of skipped sc, 10ch] to end, ss into first ss.
Fasten off.

Second side

With green, make 46ch.

Round 1: 1ss into 2nd ch from hook, [10ch, skip 1ch, 1sc into next ch] to end.

Row 2: [10ch, 1ss into skipped ch] to end.
Fasten off.

MAKING UP

Alternating colors, lay out circles in 2 rows of 5. Wrap a tab around adjoining circles and join with sc as illustrated below. Sew first side of flower fastener to one end of bracelet. Fold second side of flower fastener in half and sew along ch edge. Sew to other end of bracelet. Stitch a small cluster of seed beads on flower fastener.

1. To join the chain, lay two chain links down next to one another, with a green tab placed over the top.

2. With the crochet hook, pick up two stitches on either side of the green tab and join with double crochet.

speckled brown bracelet

Bead crochet is not often made today, but you can use it to make the most wonderful chunky jewelry. These pieces were initially inspired by the thick clusters of little round flowers on the grape hyacinths in my garden.

Materials
1 10g x ball of Presencia Finca Perle cotton No 8, beige
No. 12 steel (0.75 mm) crochet hook
Size 6 bead mix

Size
One size, to fit average adult wrist.

Gauge
Just make sure the beads are thickly clustered together.

Abbreviations
ch chain
ss slip stitch
st(s) stitch(es)

Notes
To yield 1 in. (2.5 cm) of 5 around beads in size 6 you will need to thread 5½ in. (14 cm). Bead crochet patterns are shown as tables of sequences and for the first bracelet you simply have a 5 bead repeat. To check you are doing the beading correctly, you should see the beads you are yet to do lying sideways and the beads you have done lying upwards.

BRACELET

Make a rope of beads for the bracelet following the illustrated steps for bead crochet on pages 56–57.

MAKING UP

Stitch one half of a fastener onto each end of the rope.

Continued on next page.

Notes
The top picture opposite shows how the barcelet will look if the beads are initially threaded in a totally random order.

The ginger and black beads bracelet below illustrates what happens when you follow a pattern—these beads were threaded on in a sequence of:
4,2,4,2,4,2,4,2,4,2,4,2.

For matching earrings, see page 58. They are made in exactly the same way, but as drops attached to earring backs.

Try making a necklace too—the principle is exactly the same as the bracelet, you just need more beads!

1. The perle cotton used for this project is very fine and thin, but before you purchase your beads make sure the central hole is large enough to take the thread.

2. Start by threading your beads onto the yarn. If you thread the colors in order it gives a different effect to threading them randomly (see photos of alternative effects on page 55).

3. The thread comes over the index finger, which gives you tension. Make a slip knot in the end of your thread leaving an 8 in. (20 cm) tail.

4. Chain 6, leaving one bead in each stitch.

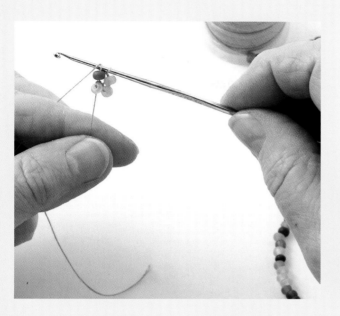

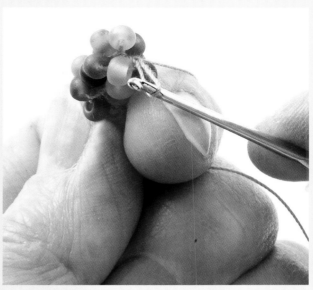

5. Pull up the row of beads to form a curve; you are aiming to get the beads on the outside. Join the chain to the first stitch with a slip stitch.

6. Flip the bead over the to the right and hold down tightly. Visually flicking the bead over is important so the bead lies to the outside and the thread to the inside.

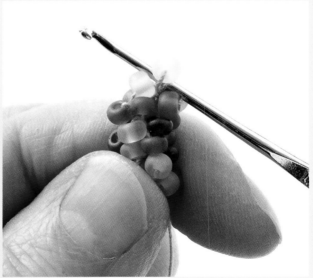

7. Pull down the next bead and catch the thread above it.

8. Pull the thread through the first loop on the hook. Pull this loop through the 2nd loop on yarn. This gives you one stitch with a bead.

variations

pink and white bracelet

The pink version of the Speckled Brown
Bracelet on page 54 uses toning shades
of pink beads for a subtle effect.

Follow the illustrated steps for bead
crochet on pages 56–57 to make this
bracelet. Here again, the beads are
initially threaded on in a random order.

metallic earrings

Metallic beads are very effective for this
type of work, and you can also use
flattened beads, as here, rather than
perfectly round ones.

When making the earrings, thread the
loose ends of the yarn at the dangling
end of the earrings up inside the beads
at the end, before trimming them off.
This will give your
earrings a neater
and more
professional
finish.

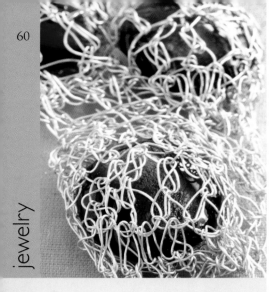

toffee drop beads

A recollection of the wonderful array of differing toffees that were available when I was a child inspired this crocheted bracelet. Each luscious bead is trapped inside a cell of champagne-colored wire—sounds good enough to eat.

Materials
1 × reel of 0.315mm champagne wire
B/1 (2.00 mm) crochet hook
6 × toffee drop glass beads from Injabulo
1 decorative clasp

Size
One size, to fit average adult wrist.

Gauge
Gauge is not important on this project.

Abbreviations
ch chain
ch sp chain space
rep repeat
sc single crochet
ss slip stitch
st(s) stitch(es)
tch turning chain

BRACELET
Leaving a 4 in. (10 cm) tail, make 12ch.
Row 1: Ch1, sc into 4th ch from hook, 1sc in each ch sp.
Row 2: 2tch, 1sc into each front loop of previous row.
Rows 3–4: As Row 2.
Enclose each glass piece within its own little wire cell and fasten the three sides by using the wire as stitching thread and working an overhand stitch. See page 62 for illustrated steps.

MAKING UP
Place the pieces in two staggered rows and join the cells up with small crocheted links. See page 62 for illustrated steps.

LINKS
Row 1: Insert hook into top of wire cell, 3sc across top.
Row 2: 2tch, 1sc in each space. Close off through top loops and bottom loops of next cell, using ss as shown in step 3 on page 62. Attach clasp using fine wire to stitch onto either end.

Continued on the next page.

Luscious toffee-color beads trapped in a delicate cage of fine wire look good enough to eat

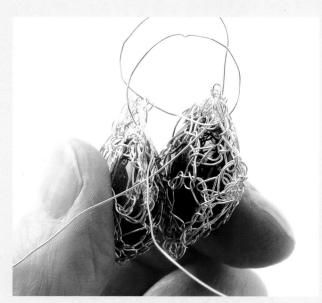

1. Place a stone on top of one square of mesh. Fold the mesh round the stone.

2. Join the open sides by "stitching" with wire.

3. Close off the links through the top loops and bottom loops of the next cell, using slip stitch as shown.

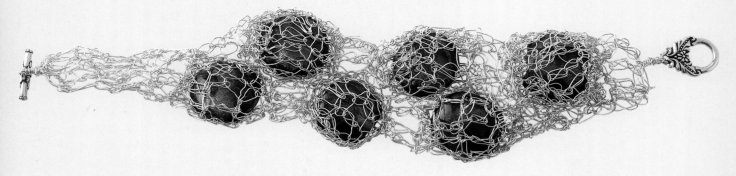

quick crochet

mosspath bracelet

Some time ago I studied moss and lichen for a textile exam, and it inspired this bracelet—as well as working with this amazing yarn. See also the brooch variation of this bracelet shown on page 65.

Materials

1 × 50g balls of NoroGanpi Abaka Surabu, color 62
No. 6 steel (1.75 mm) crochet hook
2 × mineral agate disks with central hole

Size

One size, to fit average adult wrist.

Gauge

Just make sure the beads are thickly clustered together.

Abbreviations

ch chain
ch sp chain space
dc double crochet
sc single crochet
ss slip stitch
st(s) stitch(es)

Continued on the next page.

RECTANGLE

(Make 3)
Make 5ch, ss in first ch to form a ring.
Round 1: 1ch, [1sc into ring, 2ch, 2sc into ring] 4 times, ss into first sc.
Round 2: Ss into 2ch sp, 3ch, 2dc into same 2ch sp, 5ch, 3sc into next 2ch sp, 5ch, 3dc into next 2ch sp, 5ch, 3sc into next 2ch sp, 5ch, ss into top of 3ch.

Round 3: Working into back loop of each st, work 1sc into each st, working 2sc into center of 5ch at each corner. Fasten off.

MAKING UP

Using a sewing needle and Noro yarn, stitch the mineral pieces to the yarn pieces as shown. Attach clasp to the end of the mineral stones.

NOTES

The bracelet consists of three identical rectangles with differing stone rings placed in between, as shown in the picture.
Take care not to wet too much.

1. The rectangles are worked mainly in single crochet: insert the hook under the second chain from hook, yarn over hook and pull through, yarn over again and pull through remaining two loops on hook.

2. With double crochet, yarn over hook, insert hook under fourth chain from hook, yarn over and pull one loop through, yarn over, draw through first two loops on hook, yarn over again and pull through remaining two loops on hook.

3. To add the stone rings to the bracelet, thread the end of the yarn through the center of the ring to attach it to the crochet as shown.

4. For the brooch variation, sew the stone ring to the center of the crochet sqaure with evenly-spaced stitches round the entire ring.

The matching brooch is made with four rectangles joined in a "flower" shape as shown above—although you could arrange them differently if you prefer. Stitch one of the mineral rings into the center of the brooch for added interest and to introduce an attractive contrast in texture.

The wonderful Noro yarn that is used for this project includes paper fiber in its composition, so take care not to get the jewelry too wet when you are wearing it.

A matching necklace is very simple to make—just follow the instructions for the bracelet but make more rectangles. Remember that you will also need more yarn and more mineral rings for the necklace than are specified for the bracelet.

summer extravaganza bracelet

This glorious bracelet is made of a rich cluster of brightly-colored irregular glass beads. The strange shapes of the beads add a random texture to the piece.

Materials
1 x 10g ball of Presencia Finca Perle cotton, No 8
B/1 (2.00 mm) crochet hook
Approx 200 irregular glass beads in assorted colors, shapes and sizes
2 springs
2 crimp beads
2 end connectors with 3/1 holes
Short length of chain
Lobster clasp

Size
One size, to fit average adult wrist.

Gauge
Just make sure the beads are thickly clustered together.

Abbreviations
ch   chain
rep   repeat

1. Make 1ch, slide 3 beads up to hook.

2. Take hook to far side of 3 beads, 1ch.

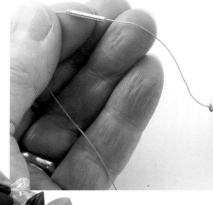

3. At the end, put on a spring—this stops the cotton fraying.

4. Add a silver crimp bead after the spring with pliers as shown.

5. Thread the spare end of the yarn through the clasp.

6. Stitch the thread onto the clasp with a backstitch. Add a drop of glue to keep the clasp firmly fixed.

Materials
1 x 50g ball of Presencia Finca Perle cotton No 8, color 0007, black
1 x 50g ball of Presencia Finca Perle cotton No 8, color 8742, taupe
1 x 50g ball of Presencia Finca Perle cotton No 8, color 8756, dark gray
1 x 50g ball of Presencia Finca Perle cotton No 8, color 8767, silver gray
1 x 50g ball of Twilleys Crochet cotton, silky white
B/1 (2.00 mm) crochet hook
4 buttons

Size
This is worked as a continuous spiral so the size can be whatever you wish.

Gauge
Gauge is not important on this project.

Abbreviations
ch chain
cont continue
dc double crochet
patt pattern
rep repeat
RS right side
sc single crochet
ss slip stitch
st(s) stitch(es)
tog together
tr treble

Notes
Make four spirals, two large (approx 3¹/₂ in. (9 cm)) and two medium (approx 2¹/₄ in. (5.5cm)), with one black, one white, one dark gray and one dark gray and taupe together.

dales gray necklet

This dramatic necklet is made of four crochet circles in different sizes and shades, which are linked and then fastened by an attached mesh collar trimmed with a border of single crochet in a contrasting yarn.

SPIRALS
Make 2ch, work 6dc into 2nd ch from hook, ss into first dc.
Cont as foll until spiral is chosen size:
1ch, work 1dc into same st as ss, 3ch, [1dc into next dc, 3ch] 5 times, [1dc into next dc, 1dc into next sp, 3ch] 6 times, [miss 1dc, 1dc into next dc, 2dc into next sp, 3ch] 6 times, [miss 1dc, 1dc into each of next 2dc, 2dc into next sp, 4ch] 6 times, [miss 1dc, 1dc into each of next 3dc, 2dc into next 4ch sp, 4ch] 6 times, [miss 1dc, 1dc into each of next 4dc, 2dc into next 4ch sp, 5ch] 6 times, [miss 1dc, 1dc into each of next 5dc, 2dc into next 5ch sp, 5ch] 6 times, [miss 1dc, 1dc into each of next 6dc, 2dc into next 5ch sp, 6ch] 6 times, [miss 1dc, 1dc into each of next 7dc, 2dc into next 6ch sp, 6ch] 6 times, [miss 1dc, 1dc into each of next 8dc, 2dc into next 6ch sp, 7 ch] 6 times.
Fasten off when size is achieved.
Sew spirals tog as in photograph.

MESH COLLAR
Using silver gray make 18ch.
Buttonhole row: 1sc into 2nd ch from hook, [3ch, miss 3ch, 1sc into next ch] 4 times, turn.
Cont in patt:
Row 1: 7ch, miss first sc, [1tr into next sc, 3ch] 3 times, 1tr into last sc, turn.
Row 2: 7ch, miss first tr, [1tr into next tr, 3ch] 3 times, 1tr into 4th of 7ch, turn.

Rep Row 2 until band measures 6¹/₄ in. (16 cm). Cont in patt joining band to spirals:
Row 1: Patt to end, 12ch, 1sc into corner of top left-hand spiral, turn.
Row 2: 12ch, 1tr into tr, patt to end.
Row 3: Patt to end, 10ch, 1sc into opp corner of same spiral, 3ch, 1sc into same spiral a few sts from last sc, turn.
Row 4: 10ch, 1tr into next tr, patt to end.
Spread next 4 joins irregularly along top right-hand spiral.
Row 5: Patt to end, 8ch, 1sc into corner of spiral, turn.
Row 6: 8ch, 1tr into tr, patt to end.
Row 7: Patt to end, 6ch, 1sc into spiral, 1ch, 1sc into spiral, turn.
Row 8: 6ch, 1tr into tr, patt to end.
Row 9: Patt to end, **10ch, 1sc into spiral, turn.
Row 10: 1ch, miss 1ch, [1dc into next ch, 2ch, miss 2ch] 3 times, 1tr into next tr, patt to end.
Patt 2 rows.
Rows 13 and 14: As Rows 9 and 10.
Patt until band fits quite tightly round neck.
Next row: 1sc into each st, turn.
Work 3 rows sc for button band.
Fasten off.
With RS facing, join black to Row 9 of band at point marked **. Work sc round outer edge of band, ending at point where Row 1 joins first spiral.
Fasten off and sew on buttons.

accessories

These accessories have been a marvelous opportunity to work with yarn on a range of smaller items. They are all part of a collection of designs dreamt up after seeing exciting new yarns and deciding to run with them.

The projects in this chapter include a great selection of unusual and eyecatching bags, cushions that will not squash down, a chunky diary cover for him—and a fluffy one for her as well. The Travel Slippers and Hot Water Bottle Cover are perfect for luxurious moments when you are far away from home. And the cute little Pixie Purse can be whatever you want it to be: a small change purse; a lipstick-only bag; or lent to your favorite little daughter for those "grown up" moments.

Whatever you choose to make, I hope you will enjoy the creative process as much as I have enjoyed designing all these great new projects.

Materials
3 x 50g balls of Patons Inca color 7006, green gray
J/10 (6.00 mm) crochet hook
2 in. (5 cm) diameter button

Size
To fit diaries: 6in (15cm) wide x 8½in (21cm) deep.

Gauge
11 sts x 12 rows to 2 in. (5 cm) square over pattern, using J/10 (6.00 mm) hook.

Abbreviations
ch chain
ch sp chain space
dc double
rep repeat
RS right side
sc single crochet
st(s) stitch(es)

Special abbreviations
1dc/rf—work 1dc round stem of next st 2 rows below, inserting hook round stem from right to left to draw up loop.

his diary cover

This chunky diary cover in a masculine natural green-gray yarn is just perfect for the men. The big wooden button is fine for male hands—no fiddly little catches to deal with here! The cover is designed to fit a standard size of diary, but check the dimensions before you begin—it's easy to adjust the size as you work if you need a bigger or smaller cover.

HIS DIARY COVER
Using J/10 (6.00 mm) hook, make 55ch.
Row 1 (RS): 1 sc into 2nd ch from hook, 1sc into each ch to end, turn. (53 sc)
Row 2: 1ch, 1sc into each sc to end, turn.
Row 3: 1 ch, 1sc into each of first 2sc, *1dc/rf round next sc 2 rows below, 1sc into each of next 2sc; rep from * to end, turn.
Row 4: 1ch, 1sc into each st to end, turn.
Row 5: 1ch, 1sc into each of first 2sc, *1dc/rf round stem of next dc/rf 2 rows below, 1sc into each of next 2 sc; rep from * to end, turn.
Rep Rows 4 and 5 until work measures 8¾ in. (22 cm).
Fasten off.

STRAP
Using J/10 (6.00 mm) hook, make 7ch.

Row 1: 1sc into 2nd ch from hook, 1sc into each ch to end, turn. (6 sc)
Row 2: 1ch, 1sc into each sc to end, turn.
Rep Row 2 until strap is long enough to stretch round diary, approx 14 in. (36 cm).
Next row (buttonhole row): 1ch, 1sc into first 2sc, 2ch, skip 2sc, 1sc into each of next 2sc, turn.
Next row: 1ch, 1sc into first 2sc, 2sc into 2ch space, 1sc into next 2sc, turn.
Work a further 4 rows of sc as set. Fasten off.

MAKING UP
Leaving 3 in. (7.5 cm) for flap, fold remainder of width over and join both sides. Sew the button to front with its center 2 in. (5 cm) from folded edge. Sew strap to back 2 in. (5 cm) from fold with long end facing toward flap.

A chunky diary cover in a cool green gray with a big wooden button—no fiddly little catches to deal with here

her diary cover

This fluffy marble diary cover with its big rose button fastener couldn't be more feminine, but if this is not your color the yarn is available in a variety of other shades. Always try and find the perfect button for your project, or create one with beads or crochet—finishing touches like this do make a big difference to the final look.

Materials
3 x 50g balls of Anny Blatt Vega color 368, marble
G/6 (4.50 mm) crochet hook
2 in. (5 cm) rose button

Size
To fit diaries: 6 in. (15 cm) wide × 8½ in. (21 cm) deep.

Gauge
7dc × 3 rows to 2 in. (5 cm) square over pattern, using G/6 (4.50 mm) hook.

Abbreviations
ch chain
ch sp chain space
dc double crochet
foll following
rep repeat
RS right side
sc single crochet
st(s) stitch(es)
WS wrong side

HER DIARY COVER

Using G/6 (4.50 mm) hook, make 65ch.
Row 1 (RS): 1dc into 4th ch from hook, 1dc into each ch to end. (63 dc)
Row 2: 3ch, 1dc into each dc to end, working into back loop only, 1dc into top of 3ch, turn.
Row 3: 3ch, 1dc into each dc to end, working into front loop only, 1dc into top of 3ch, turn.
Rep Rows 2 and 3 until the work measures 8¾ in. (22 cm).
Fasten off.

STRAP

Using G/6 (4.50 mm) hook and B, make 7ch.
Row 1: 1sc into 2nd ch from hook, 1sc into each ch to end. (6 sc)
Row 2: 1ch, 1sc into each sc to end, turn.

Rep Row 2 until strap is long enough to stretch round diary, approx 14 in. (36 cm).
Next row (buttonhole row): 1ch, 1sc into first 2sc, 2ch, skip 2sc, 1sc into each of next 2sc, turn.
Next row: 1ch, 1sc into first 2sc, 2sc into 2ch sp, 1sc into next 2sc, turn.
Work 6 rows sc.
Fasten off.

MAKING UP

Leaving 4¼ in. (11 cm) for flap, fold remainder of width over and join both sides. Sew end of strap on back 2 in. (5 cm) from folded edge, with long end of strap facing away from flap. Sew the button on back above strap.

Fluffy yarn makes a super-feminine diary cover—just the thing to bring a bit of romance into your life

Materials
6 × 50g balls of Karaoke, red multi
F/5 (4.00 mm) crochet hook
E/4 (3.50 mm) crochet hook

Size
After felting: 13¹/₂ in. (34 cm) wide; 12 in (30 cm) deep, excluding handles.
Before felting: 19¹/₂ in. (49 cm) wide; `
18¹/₂ in. (46 cm) deep.

Gauge
16dc × 8 rows to 4 in. (10 cm) over double crochet using E/4 (3.50 mm) hook, before felting.

Abbreviations
ch chain
dc double crochet
rep repeat
RS right side
sc single crochet
ss slip stitch
st(s) stitch(es)
WS wrong side

Special abbreviations
dc2tog—double crochet 2 together, wrap yarn over hook, insert hook into next st, wrap yarn over hook, draw a loop through, wrap yarn and draw through 2 loops on hook, (2 loops left on hook), rep into next st, (3 loops on hook), wrap yarn and draw through 3 loops on hook to complete.

felted weekend tote

The tote is "this year's" bag and, when I saw this yarn, I designed the bag for it—which is opposite to how I normally work, but I was really excited by the possibilities. This bag will take you from shopping to weekends away.

BAG
(worked as one piece)
Using F/5 (4.00 mm) hook, make 176ch, join with ss into first ch to form a circle. Change to E/4 (3.50 mm) hook.
Round 1 (RS): 3ch, (count as first st), 1dc into each ch to end, ss into top of 3ch. (176 sts)
Round 2: 3ch, (count as first st), 1dc into each dc to end, ss in top of 3ch. Rep this last round until work measures 13 in. (32 cm).
Divide for handles.
Row 1: **2ch, skip first st, 1dc into next st (this counts as dc2tog), 1dc into each of next 17dc, dc2tog over next 2sts, turn. (19 sts)
Row 2: 1ch, 1sc into first st, 1dc into each of next 18 sts, turn. (19 sts)
Rep this last row a further 13 times. Fasten off. **
Skip next 37dc, rejoin yarn with a sl st into next st, repeat from ** to **.
Skip next 9dc, rejoin yarn with a sl st into next st, repeat from ** to **.
Skip next 37dc, rejoin yarn with a sl st into next st, repeat from ** to **.
9dc left unworked.

MAKING UP
With RS of bag facing, fold each handle in half lengthways, continuing to fold to lower edge of bag, pin together (this makes it easier to crochet together). To form folds at either side of bag, with RS facing, using F/5 (4.00 mm) hook and working through all 4 thicknesses, join top of 1st and 4th handles together by working 1 row of sc across folded handles. Fasten off. Join other 2 handles. Working through all 4 thicknesses at each end, and double thickness at center, work 1 row of sc across lower edge of bag. Fasten off.

FELTING
To felt the bag, wear rubber gloves. Fill a bowl with hot water and put the bag into it. Leave for 10 mins, allowing the fibers to soak up the hot water. Add a little soap powder and stir round, dissolving the powder. Empty out some of the water and top up again with hot water; some dye may come out of the yarn, but do not worry. Squeeze and pummel the bag repeatedly so the yarn gets fluffier. Take the bag out occasionally and squeeze out excess water. Lay it flat and measure. If it is still too big, repeat the process again. When you have finished felting, put the bag into cold water and squeeze gently, then put it into a washing machine on a short spin cycle. Take out bag and pull back into shape, if needed. Place onto a towel and dry.

pixie purse

The smallest bag—a fun bag for the loose change in your main bag, or how about just a lipstick and credit card when you go out dancing! The delicious yarns available today just cry out to be bought and worked into something, but often it's a problem to find something to make with just one hank or ball. Well here is Pixie, a delight to suit any age group and to show off that chosen yarn to perfection.

Materials
1 x 50g hank of Noro Daria, color 6
B/1 (2.00 mm) crochet hook
1 x 3 in. (7.5 cm) purse frame from www.u-handbag.com
Fabric glue

Size
Width 4 in. (10 cm); depth 3¹/₄ in. (8 cm).

Gauge
20 sts x 9 rows to 4 in. (10 cm) using B/1 (2.00 mm) crochet hook.

Abbreviations
ch chain
dc double crochet
RS right side
ss slip stitch
st(s) stitch(es)
WS wrong side
yoh yarn over hook

Special abbreviations
dc2tog—double crochet 2 together, wrap yarn over hook, insert hook into next st, wrap yarn over hook, draw loop through, wrap yarn and draw through 2 loops on hook (2 loops left on hook); rep this step into next st (3 loops on hook), wrap yarn and draw through 3 loops on hook.

PURSE
Make 54ch. Worked with WS facing. Work into back loop of each st throughout.
Round 1: 2ch, 1dc into each ch, ss in top of 2ch.
Round 2: 2ch, 1dc into each dc, ss into top of 2ch.
Rep last round 4 times.
Round 7: 3ch, 1dc into each of next 3dc, dc2tog, [4dc, dc2tog] to end, ss in top of 2ch. (45 sts)
Fasten off.
Base
Rejoin yarn to first ch of foundation ch, 2ch, 1dc into each of next 17ch, turn. (18 sts)

Work 4 rows in dc.
Fasten off.

MAKING UP
Sew base in place. Turn the entire bag to RS.
Place 3 in. (7.5 cm) purse frame into bag, with short side tops into the slits under the clasp and the hinged side fitting outside the sides.
Using fabric glue, coat both sides of the work and glue into frame groove. Push into place and hold for a few minutes, then place in cool place to dry firm.

Tips

● Using a purchased frame like the one in this project is an ideal way to make your finished item look professional. There is a wide range of types available from craft or yarn stores—or you can try the internet.

● The look of this purse can be changed by using a different frame, some of which have optional long chains so you can use the purse as a tiny shoulder bag.

● If you don't want to use glue to attach the purse to the frame, make sure you buy a frame with holes for stitching.

The Pixie Purse is perfect
for life's little essentials

bramble bag

A small wild bramble found giving forth its fruit in late summer—picked and eaten with fresh pouring cream—was the starting point for this design. The shape was taken from the wide base of the bramble, which narrowed as it climbed to find the sun for its fruits. The button is, of course, the largest bramble—which is always out of reach. A fun design to remind me of summer.

Materials
2 x 50g balls of
Louisa Harding Impressions, color 06
1 large button
C/2 (3.00 mm) crochet hook

Size
Width 8¹/₂ in. (22 cm); depth 6 in. (15 cm).

Gauge
20sc to 4 in. (10 cm) on C/2 (3.00 mm) hook.

Abbreviations
dc double crochet
sc single crochet
yoh yarn over hook

Special abbreviations
sc2tog—insert hook into next st, yoh, draw a loop through; rep into the next st, yoh, draw through all loops on hook.
dc2tog—yoh, insert hook into next st, yoh, draw a loop through, yoh, draw through 2 loops on hook; rep into next st, yoh, draw through all loops on hook.

FRONT

Make 46ch.
Row 1: 1sc into 2nd ch from hook, 1sc into each ch to end. (45 sc)
Row 2: 1ch, 1sc into first sc, sc2tog, 1sc into each sc to end.
Rep last row unil 23 sts remain. Cont straight until work measures 4³/₄ in. (12 cm).
Fasten off.

BACK

Work as front but do not fasten off.

FLAP

Row 1: 3ch (counts as first dc), skip first st, dc2tog, 1dc into each st to last 3 sts, dc2tog, 1dc into last st, turn.
Rep last row until 5 sts remain.
Next row: 3ch, [dc2tog] twice, turn.
Next row: 2ch, dc2tog, yoh and drawn through 2 loops. Work a 12 in. (30 cm) length of ch on remaining loop.
Fasten off.

STRAP

Make 4ch, ss into first ch to form a ring. Work 5sc into ring, then work in continuous rounds of sc until strap measures 14 in. (35 cm).
Fasten off.

MAKING UP

Join sides of bag. Work ch loops along lower edge. [10ch, ss into each of next 2 sts] all round, varying no of ch in loops.
Fasten off.
Turn bag inside out and join lower straight edge leaving ch loops free. Turn to RS. Stitch the strap to the bag, making coil at one side to form a small circle.
Stitch large button to front using length of ch at end of flap to fasten bag.

Inspired by a late-fruiting bramble, this is a fun design to remind me of the summer

bobble bag

Think of hazy summer days, the soft green fields in the sun, lazy evenings—the textures and colors in this little bag bring back these wonderful memories.

Materials

1 × 50g ball of Rowan Summer Tweed, rush (A)
1 × mixed hank of Stef Francis embroidery thread, color 07 (B)
F/5 (4.00 mm) crochet hook
Handle from www.u-handbag.com

Size

Width 7½ in. (19 cm); depth 6 in. (15 cm)

Gauge

15 sts × 12 rows to 4 in. (10 cm) over patt using G/6 (4.00 mm) hook.

Abbreviations

dc double crochet
sc single crochet
ss slip stitch
st(s) stitch(es)
yoh yarn over hook

Special abbreviations

sc2tog—insert hook into next st, yoh, draw a loop through; rep into the next st, yoh, draw through all loops on hook.
MB—make bobble, leaving last loop of each dc on hook work 5dc into back loop of next st, yoh and draw through all 6 loops.

FRONT

Using 1 strand of each yarn together, make 30ch.
    Row 1: 1sc into 2nd ch from hook, 1sc into each ch to end, turn. (29 sc)
Row 2: 3ch, skip first sc, working into back loops work 1dc into next sc, [MB in next sc, 1dc into each of next 2sc] to end, turn.
Row 3: 1ch, working into front loops work 1sc into first dc, 1sc into each st to end, turn.
Row 4: As Row 2.
Row 5: As Row 3 working sc2tog 3 times evenly accross. (3 sts decreased)
Row 6: As Row 2.
Rows 7 and 8: As Rows 3 and 4.
Rows 9–16: Work Rows 5 and 6 four times, varying positions of sc2tog on each dec row.
Work 6 rows sc.
Fasten off.

BACK

Using A only, work as front.

BOBBLE

Using A only, make 4ch, 12dc into 4th ch from hook, ss into top of 3ch.
Next row: 2ch, [leaving last loop of each dc on hook work 1dc into each of next 4dc, yoh and draw through all 5 loops] 3 times, 6ch.
Fasten off.
Stuff bobble with scraps of yarn, then join in opening.

MAKING UP

Leaving top 2¼ in. (6 cm) open at each side, join sides and lower edge. Fold top 3 rows of back and front over a handle and sew down. Join ch of bobble to top of one side.

The textures and colors in this bag remind me of lazy summer days in the sun

Materials
4 x 50g balls of Adriafil Graphic
E/4 (3.50 mm) crochet hook
Large button
Magnetic bag catch

Size
Width: 12¹/₂ in. (31 cm); depth 7 in.
(18 cm).

Gauge
14 sc x 17 rows to 4 in. (10 cm) using E/4
(3.50 mm) hook.

Abbreviations
alt alternate
ch chain
cont continue
dc double crochet
dec decrease
inc increase
rep repeat
RS right side
sc single crochet
ss slip stitch
st(s) stitch(es)
tch turning chain
WS wrong side

Special abbreviations
sc2tog—single crochet 2 sts together,
insert hook into next st, wrap yarn over
hook, draw a loop through; rep this step
into the next st (3 loops on the hook),
yarn over hook and draw through all
3 loops on the hook to complete.
dc2tog—double crochet 3 sts together,
wrap yarn over hook, insert hook into next
st, wrap yarn over hook, draw a loop
through, wrap yarn and draw through 2 of
loops on hook (2 loops left on hook); rep
this step into next st (3 loops on hook),
wrap yarn and draw through all 3 loops on
hook to complete.

retro clutch bag

This glorious yarn just called out to me, asking to be made
into something unusual and desirable. Here is a great little
clutch bag with retro styling, which makes the best of its
textures and colors. It's made in one piece, so there is minimal
sewing to do at the end.

BAG
(Worked in one piece)
Front
Make 37ch.
Row 1: 1sc into 2nd ch from hook,
1sc into each ch to end, turn. (36 sc)
Row 2: 1ch, 1sc into each st to end,
turn.
Rep last row once more.
Row 3 (inc row): 1ch, 1sc into first
st, 2sc into next st, 1sc into each st to
last 2 sts, 2sc into next st, 1sc into
last st, turn.
Work 5 rows sc.
Rep last 6 rows 3 times. (44 sc)
Mark each end of last row.
Cont straight until work measures
7 in. (18 cm).
Mark each end of last row.
Gussets
Leave main piece of work, cut a
length of yarn and attach tp tch of
last row, make 28ch.
Fasten off.
Cont with main yarn.
Next row: Make 29ch, 1sc into 2nd
ch from hook, 1sc into each ch, 1sc
into each sc of main bag, 1sc into
each ch to end, turn. (100 sc)
Work in sc until gusset measures
2 in. (5 cm).
Fasten off.
Next row: Skip first 28sc, rejoin yarn
to next sc, 1ch, 1sc into this st and
foll 43 sts, turn. (44 sc)

Work straight in sc for the same
number of rows (or the same
measurement) as between markers
on front.
Work a further 3 rows as set.
Next row (dec row): 1ch, 1sc in first
sc, sc2tog over next 2 sts, 1sc into
each st to last 3 sts, sc2tog over next
2 sts, 1sc into last st, turn.
Work 5 rows of sc.
Rep last 6 rows 3 times. (36 sts)
Cont straight until work measures
16 in. (41 cm), dec 4 sts evenly across
last row. (32 sts)
Front flap
Every row is worked with RS
facing—do not turn at end of rows.
Row 1: 3ch (count as 1dc), skip first
st, 1dc into each st to end. (32 sts)
Row 2: Work from left to right
working into front loop of each st,
*7ch, ss into next dc; rep from *
ending 7ch, ss into top of 3ch.
Row 3 (inc row): 3ch, (count as
1dc), skip first dc, working into back
loops of last dc row work 2dc into
next st, *1dc into each st to last 2 sts,
2dc into next st, 1dc into last st. (34
dc)
Row 4: As Row 2.
Rep last 2 rows once more. (36 sts)
Row 7: 3ch (count as 1dc), skip first
st, working into back loops of last dc
row work 1dc into each st.
Row 8: As Row 2.

Tips

- The button on the front of this bag is just for show—it closes with a magnetic fastening that is attached behind. Choose a very decorative button in quite a large size for best effect.

- This yarn has the most wonderful texture and comes in a range of exciting colors. It is not that easy to work with at first but persevere—the results are more than worth the effort.

- You can line this bag if you wish—use the finished crochet piece as a "pattern" to cut the fabric, but remember to allow extra all round for the seams. The magnetic catch can either be stitched in place on the lining, or you can stitch it in place first so the lining covers it; the magnet should be strong enough to work through a thin layer of fabric.

Rep last 2 rows once more.

Flap shaping

Row 1: 3ch (count as 1dc), skip first st, working into back loops of last dc row work dc2tog over next 2 sts, 1dc into next 12 sts, dc2tog over next 2 sts, 1dc into next st. (16 sts) Work on these sts only.

Row 2: As Row 2 of main flap pattern.

Dec in this way on next and foll 2 alt rows.

Work 2nd row again.

Fasten off.**

With RS facing, rejoin yarn to first st after first side and work from ** to **.

MAKING UP

With RS together, sew gussets in place. Turn to RS. Sew button to center of flap shaping.

Attach the magnetic fastening behind the button, by stitching each half to a circle of stiff fabric first, then stitch this to the inside of the bag to correspond with the button position.

going to tea bag

Scenes from nature and architecture often inspire me and the "going to tea" bag shape came from a circular staircase in a hotel where I stayed once, in the county of Yorkshire in northern England.

Materials
1 × 50g ball of Debbie Bliss Maya, soft green (A)
1 × 50g ball of Colinette Enigma, green (B)
1 × rose handle from u-handbags.com
F/5 (4.00 mm) crochet hook

Size
Width 9 in. (23 cm); depth 7 in. (18 cm).

Gauge
Gauge is not important for this project.

Abbreviations
ch chain
dc double crochet
hdc half double
sc single crochet
tr treble
ss slip stitch

BACK

Using A, make 4ch, ss into first ch to form a ring.
Work 8sc into ring.
Cont in a spiral, working into back loop of each st. 1hdc into each of 5sc, 2dc into each of next 13 sts, 2tr into each of next 7 sts, *1tr into next st, 2tr into next st; rep from * until bag measures 7 in. (18 cm) across.
Fasten off.

FRONT

Work as back using 1 strand A and B together.

FRILL

With back facing, join back and front together, working into both loops of back and back loop of front.
4ch, *2tr into next st, 1tr into next st; rep from * round just over half of outer edge.
Fasten off.

MAKING UP

Backstitch through both thicknesses at base of frill. Turn over top edge to form a straight line. Attach handles as per manufacturer's instructions.

Tips

● Using two strands of yarn together is great to add more texture and bulk to your projects. Always make sure the yarns blend or contrast in color and have differing textures for more effect.

● Sewing the bag together with slip stitch is a quick and easy way of making it up and is the best method for this design and the edge wanted.

● When choosing a handle check the size of the opening carefully before sewing up. The handle used for this bag, like many, needs no glueing or sewing—it uses clasps to hold the crochet.

● Always keep interesting handles from old bags to reuse in your new designs.

zig zag bag

The architecture of Barcelona, with its well-defined shapes and colors, gave me the first ideas for this bag. Colors from comic books provided the rest of my inspiration. Great fun to make and use!

Materials

1 × 100g ball of South West Trading Optimum DK, color 560, bubble gum (A)
1 × 100g ball of Bouton d'Or Flash, serpolet (B)
1 × 100g ball of Ironstone Glisseen, color ng/7 (C)
E/4 (3.50 mm) crochet hook
Decorative rose button
Magnetic catch

Size

Width: 7 in. (18 cm); depth 5¹/₂ in. (14 cm).

Gauge

1 patt rep of 16 sts measures 3¹/₂ in. (9 cm)
wide using E/4 (3.50 mm) crochet hook.

Abbreviations

ch chain
ch sp chain space
cont continue
dc double crochet
patt pattern
rep repeat
sc single crochet
st(s) stitch(es)
tr treble
yoh yarn over hook

Special abbreviations

dc3tog—wrap yarn over hook, insert hook into next st, wrap yarn over hook, draw a loop through, wrap yarn and draw through 2 loops on hook (2 loops left on hook); rep this step into next st (3 loops on hook), rep this step into next st (4 loops on hook), wrap yarn and draw through all four loops on hook to complete.

BACK AND FRONT ALIKE

Using A, make 36ch.
Row 1: Using A, 1dc into 4th ch from hook, *1dc into each of next 6ch, dc3tog over next 3ch, 1dc into each of next 6ch, *[1dc, 1ch, 1dc] into next ch; rep from * to * once, 2dc into last ch, turn.
Row 2: Using B, 3ch, work into front loop of each st, 1dc into first dc, *1dc into each of next 6dc, dc3tog over next 3sts, 1dc into each of next 6dc, *[1dc, 1ch, 1dc] in 1ch sp; rep from * to * once more, 2dc in 3rd of 3ch, turn.
Row 3: Using C, 3ch, work into back loop of each st, 1dc into first dc, *1dc into each of next 6dc, dc3tog over next 3sts, 1dc into each of next 6dc, *[1dc, 1ch, 1dc] in 1ch sp; rep from * to * once, 2dc in 3rd of 3ch, turn.

Rows 2 and 3 form patt.
Cont in patt in stripes of 2 rows A, [1 row C, 1 row A] twice, 2 rows C and 1 row B.
Fasten off.
Join sides and base.

HANDLE

Using A and C tog, make 4ch, ss in first ch to form a ring.
5sc into ring.
Work in continuous rounds of ss, working into front loop only of each st, until handle measures 8¹/₂ in. (22 cm).
Fasten off.

EDGING

Using C.
First petal: *4ch, skip 3ch, [3dc, 3ch, 1ss] in next ch;

The well-defined shapes and the colors of the architecture of Barcelona has inspired this fun bag

2nd petal: 5ch, skip 3ch, [1dc, 3tr, 1dc, 3ch, 1ss] in next ch;
3rd petal: 5ch, skip 3ch, [3dc, 3ch, 1ss] in next ch; 6ch; rep from *until edging fits along base, omitting 6ch at end of last rep.
Fasten off.
Make another strip to match.

MAKING UP

Sew edging strips to base of bag. Sew handle in place. Sew button to center top of front and use ch sp of center top of back as buttonhole.

Tips

● If you do not want to use a crochet cord for this bag there are many different types of handle available from specialist websites such as u-handbags.com or bagsofhandles.co.uk.

● The rose button used in this project is a special one chosen for this bag. Look out for interesting buttons in specialist stores and on internet sites.

● The button is decorative—the bag is secured with a magnetic catch stitched inside. If you want to use the button but do not want to make a buttonhole in the flap, make a short crochet chain to slip over the button instead.

Materials
4 × 50g balls of Lana Grossa Pashmina, color 14, gray (A)
1 × 50g ball of Lana Grossa Pashmina, color 05, pink (B)
F/5 (4.00 mm) crochet hook
E/4 (3.50 mm) crochet hook

Size
To fit an average hot water bottle: width: 11½ in. (29 cm); length 15 in. (38 cm), including top gathering.

Gauge
20sc × 26 rows to 4 in. (10 cm) over double crochet, using F/5 (4.00 mm) hook.

Abbreviations
ch chain
ch sp chain space
dc double crochet
RS right side
sc single crochet
ss slip stitch
st(s) stitch(es)
tog together
WS wrong side

hot water bottle cover

There's nothing so warm and cosy on a cold winter's night as being able to snuggle up to a toasty hot water bottle. And here is the perfect cover to make your bottle look smart and sophisticated enough for any inspection!

FRONT AND BACK
(both alike)
Using F/5 (4.00 mm) hook and MC, make 59ch.
Row 1 (RS): 1sc into 2nd ch from hook, 1sc into each ch to end, turn. (58 sc)
Next row: 1ch, 1sc into each sc to end, turn.
Rep last row until work measures 2 in. (5 cm), ending with a WS row.
**Change to B, do not cut A but carry it up side of work.
Work two rows sc in B.
Cut off B.**
Cont in A until work measures 8¾ in. (22 cm), ending with a WS row.
Work from ** to **.
Cont in A until work measures 11 in. 28 cm), ending with a WS row.

Eyelet row: 3ch (count as 1dc), skip first sc, 1dc into next sc, [1ch, skip next sc, 1dc into each of next 3sc] to end.
Next row: 1ch, 1sc into each dc and each ch sp, ending with 1sc into top of 3ch, turn.
Cont in sc until work measures 15 in. (38 cm).
Fasten off.

MAKING UP
With RS tog, using E/4 (3.50 mm) hook, join A to top of side edge. Join sides and lower edge by working 1 row of sc through both thicknesses. Turn to RS.
Top edging
Using E/4 (3.50 mm) hook and A, starting at top side seam and working all round top edge, work the foll: 1ch, [1sc, 3ch, 1sc] into first sc, *skip next sc, [1sc, 3ch, 1sc] into next sc; rep from * ending with skip next sc, ss into first sc.
Fasten off.

CORD
Using F/5 (4.00 mm) hook and A double, make a 40 in. (100 cm) length of ch. Working into 2nd ch from hook and each ch to end, ss back along the length of ch placing the hook into the strand on the reverse side of each ch.

Fasten off and sew in ends.
Beginning at center front, thread the
cord through the eyelets. Pull the ties
together and tie in a neat bow to
form a snug fit round the neck of the
bottle.

Materials
1 x 25g ball of Twilleys Crochet cotton, cream (A)
1 x 25g ball of Anny Blatt Victoria ribbon (B)
E/4 (3.50 mm) crochet hook

Size
Depth 5 in. (13 cm); width at lower edge 4¼ in. (11 cm).

Gauge
25 sc to 4 in. (10 cm) using E/4 (3.50 mm) crochet hook.

Abbreviations
ch chain
dc double crochet
inc increase
rep repeat
RS right side
sc single crochet
ss slip stitch
st(s) stitch(es)
WS wrong side

lavender bag

The smell of lavender is always evocative of warm summer days and there is nothing nicer than sliding between crisp cotton sheets surrounded by the delicate scent of these flowers. This little bag is decorated with a stitched ribbon flower for that perfect finishing touch.

BACK
Beg at top edge. Using E/4 (3.50 mm) hook and A, make 24ch.
Row 1 (RS): 1sc into 2nd ch from hook, 1sc to end, turn. (23 sc)
Work into back loop of st throughout.
Row 2: 1ch, 1sc into each st to end, turn.
Rep Row 2 twice.
Eyelet row: 1ch, 1sc into first sc, [1ch, skip 1sc, 1sc into next sc] to end, turn*
Rep Row 2 until work measures 3½ in. (9 cm) from beg, end with WS row.
Work 2 rows sc in B.
Next row: Carry color not in use loosely across WS. 1ch, work in sc working 4A, 5B, 5A, 5B and 4A.
**Next row (inc): With B, 1ch, 1dc into each of first 2sc, [2sc into next sc, 1sc into each of next 5sc] 3 times,

2sc into next sc, 1sc into each of last 2sc, turn. (27 sc)
Work 1 row sc with A and 2 rows B. Fasten off.

FRONT
Work as back to *.
Rep row 2 until front measures same as back to inc row. Complete as back from **.

DRAWSTRING
Using B, make a 24 in. (60 cm) length of ch. Fasten off.

MAKING UP
Using B, make chain stitch flowers on front. Join A to top left corner, 5ch, ss into corner, 7ch, ss into same place, 5ch, ss into same place. Fasten off. Join sides and lower edge from eyelet row. Thread drawstring and tie.

travel slippers

Once again the color for these pretty pumps was inspired by the plants and flowers in my own garden. The colors of the fading delphiniums in the border just sparked the idea—the clear blues of early summer change and turn a bluey lilac as the season progresses.

Materials

2 × 50g balls of Lang Soft Shetland, color 1057 (A)
Small amount of Trendsetter Merino Sie, lilac
Small amount of Trendsetter Merino Sie, olive
E/4 (3.50 mm) crochet hook
Pair of polystyrene shoe lasts

Size

To fit UK shoe size 4–5.

Gauge

Gauge is not important for this project, as the slippers are felted to fit.

Abbreviations

ch chain
ch sp chain space
dc double crochet
hdc half double
sc single crochet
ss slip stitch
st(s) stitch(es)
yoh yarn over hook

Special abbreviations

dc2tog—wrap yarn over hook, insert hook into next st, wrap yarn over hook, draw a loop through, wrap yarn and draw through 2 loops on hook (2 loops left on hook); rep this step into next st (3 loops on hook), wrap yarn and draw through all loops on hook to complete.

SOLES

(Make 2 and flip for right and left foot)
Using A, make 16ch.
Row 1: 1dc into 4th ch from hook, 1dc into each ch to end, turn. (14 sts)
Row 2: 3ch, 1dc into first dc, 1dc into each dc, 2dc into top of 3ch, turn. (16 sts)
Rows 3–4: 3ch, skip first dc, 1dc int each dc, 1dc into top of 3ch, turn.
Rows 5–6: 3ch, skip first dc, dc2tog, 1dc into each dc to last 3 sts, dc2tog, 1dc into top of 3ch, turn. (12 sts)
Rows 7–9: 3ch, 2dc in first dc, 2dc in next dc, 1dc in each dc, 1dc in top of 3ch, turn.
Row 10: 3ch, 1dc in first dc, 1dc in each dc, 1dc in top of 3ch, turn. (22 sts)
Row 11: As Row 7. (25 sts)
Row 12: As Row 10. (26 sts)
Rows 13–16: 3ch, skip first dc, 1dc in each dc, 1dc into top of 3ch, turn.
Row 18: 3ch, mist first dc, dc2tog, [1dc in next dc, 2dctog] 7 times, dc2tog. (17 sts)
Fasten off.

TOPS

(Make 2)
Work from top down towards soles.
Using A, make 71ch, ss in first ch to form a ring.

Round 1: 1sc in next 20ch, 1hdc in next 10ch, 1dc in next 5ch, [2dc, 1ch, 2dc] in next ch (this is the toe), 1dc in next 5ch, 1hdc in next 10ch, 1sc in next 20ch, ss in first sc, turn. (75 sts)
Round 2: 1ch, 1sc in next 20sc, 1hdc in next 10hdc, 1dc in next 7dc [2dc, 1ch, 2dc] in 1ch sp, 1dc in next 7dc, 1hdc in next 10hdc, 1sc in next 20 sc, ss in first sc, turn. (79 sts)
Round 3: 1ch, 1sc in next 20sc, 1hdc in next 10hdc, 1dc in next 9hdc, [2dc, 1ch, 2dc] in 1ch sp, 1dc in next 9dc, 1hdc in next 10hdc, 1sc in next 20 sc, ss in first sc, turn. (83 sts)
Round 4: 1ch, 1sc in next 20sc, 1hdc in next 10hdc, 1dc in next 11dc, [2dc, 1ch, 2dc] in 1ch sp, 1dc in next 11dc, 1hdc in next 10hdc, 1sc in next 20sc, ss in first sc, turn. (87 sts)

Notes

Yarn is used double throughout—pull one end from inside of one ball and one from outside and hold together.

The slippers will look enormous as you finish them but this is correct—they shrink down in size when felted so do not worry.

Back of heel

1sc in next 19sc, ss in next st, turn,
1sc in next 38sts, ss in next st, turn,
1sc in next 19sts.
Fasten off.

TWISTS

(Make 4 in A and 1 each in scraps of
other colors, varying length of ch
each time)
Make approx 25ch.
Row 1: Skip 1ch, 2sc in each ch.
Fasten off.

MAKING UP

Attach tops to soles by overstitching
along edges.

The bluey-lilac of late summer delphiniums inspired these pretty and oh-so-soft travel slippers

FELTING

Place the ballet slippers on the last
then put a pop sock over each one
and tie to hold everything in place.
Place the slippers in the washing
machine on a hot wash.
Try pumps on after one wash—if still
too big or not shrunk to shoe last,
give one more wash on the last.
Leave the pumps on the last until
completely dry.
Stitch twists to top of slipper.

Tips

● For successful machine felting you
will need to know your machine well.
Knit a few swatches, measure them,
then try felting at different settings to
see how much they shrink. These
slippers should shrink by 25–30%.

● The slippers can also be felted by
hand. Fill a large bowl with hot water
and soap and wear rubber gloves to
protect your hands. Immerse the item
fully. Rub gently all over the surface
with your hands, gently squeezing the
water out every so often, then begin
the process again. Repeat until the
item is the size you would like it to
be, using the polystyrene lasts for the
last stages to get the correct shape.
Be careful with any subsequent
washes, or the item may felt more
and thus shrink further.

● Use liquid soap when felting, not
detergent. Soap helps the water soak
into the fibers so they open up and
felt better.

● Place an old lint-free towel in the
machine along with the slippers to
help create more friction. Items also
felt better in the machine if they are
not enclosed in a bag.

his & hers cushion

This cushion is so easy to make but it's full of texture and vibrant color. The pattern is for a square cushion but you can make the same design into a rectangular shape if you like by working more multiples of the rows.

Materials
10 x 50g balls of Gedifra Colorito, color 6946
H/8 (5.00 mm) crochet hook
12 in. (30 cm) square pillow form

Size
12 in. (30 cm) square.

Gauge
13 sts x 20 rows to 4 in. (10 cm) over patt using H/8 (5.00 mm) hook.

Abbreviations
ch chain
patt pattern
rep repeat
RS right side
sc single crochet
st(s) stitch(es)
WS wrong side

Notes
Yarn is used double throughout, changing combinations at random, carrying yarns not in use loosely up side of work.

CUSHION FRONT AND BACK
(Both alike).
Make 41ch.
Row 1 (WS): 1sc into 2nd ch from hook, 1sc into each ch to end, turn. (40 sc)
Row 2: 1ch, 1sc into sc, turn.
Row 3: As Row 2.
Row 4: 1ch, *[1sc into sc 3 rows below next sc] 5 times, 1sc into each of next 5sc; rep from * to end, turn.

Row 5: As Row 2.
Row 6: 1ch, *1sc into each of next 5sc, [1sc into sc 3 rows below next sc] 5 times to end, turn.
Rep Rows 3 to 6 until work measures 12 in. (30 cm).
Fasten off.

MAKING UP
With RS tog, join 3 sides, turn to RS, insert pillow form then join remaining side.

Tips

● Pillow forms come in a wide variety of shapes and sizes. The pattern is designed for one 12 in. (30 cm) square, so if your cushion is bigger you will need to adjust the pattern to suit. As long as you keep making multiples of the basic pattern of 47 double crochet and 6 rows this should not be a problem. Remember that a bigger cushion will need more yarn!

● Use quite a firm pillow form for these cushions to make the most of the wonderful texture across the surface.

materials and techniques

Crochet is very versatile and all you need are a few basic materials and to know how to work the few simple stitches that in different combinations can be used to work any crochet pattern. This section gives details of everything you will need and also explains the basic techniques.

yarns & hooks

Although there are special crochet yarns available, you can crochet with any yarn suitable for knitting as well—and even with fine wire. There are beautiful materials available now—see the back of this book for suppliers.

Crochet hooks vary in size and are most often available in plastic or aluminum. Some pattern books give hook sizes in different formats, so the handy conversion chart (right) will help you find the right size.

Crochet hook conversions

Metric (mm)	US size	UK/Canada (old) Wool	Cotton
0.60	No. 14 steel	-	7
0.75	No. 12 steel	-	6½
1.00	No. 10 steel	-	5½
1.25	No. 9 steel	-	4½
1.50	No. 8 steel	16	3½
1.75	No. 7 steel	15	2½
2.00	B/1	14	1½
2.50	C/2	12	0
3.00	D/3	11	3
3.50	E/4	9	4
4.00	F/5	8	5
4.50	G/6	7	
5.00	H/8	6	
5.50	I/9	5	
6.00	J/10	4	
6.50	K10 ½	3	
7.00	K10 ½	2	
8.00	L/12	0	
9.00	M/13	00	
10.00	N/15	000	
12.00	N/15	000	
15.00	N/15	000	
17.00	N/15	000	
25.00	N/15	000	
35.00	N/15	000	

Yarn conversions

25g	⅞oz
50g	1¾oz
100g	3½oz

Yarns are listed with their NM number to describe their yardage. This number states how many meters of yarn will come from 1 gram weight, so for example a single ply 1/28 yarn will give 28 meters—or 92 feet—per gram whilst 2/28 will give half that (because it is twice as thick). The table below gives the yardage, needle sizes and stitches per inch.

Weight	(Tex)	Yards per 150g cone (approx)	Needle size, stocking stitch	Needle size, lace	US crochet hook size	Stitches per inch (guide)
lace	1/14 or 2/28 (or 70 Tex)	2,300	Many people use several strands of this together for hand knitting	US 2–5, 2.50–3.75mm, old UK 12–9	8 or 9	7–8
4 ply	2/14 (or 140 Tex)	1,150	US 0–1, 2.00–2.75mm, old UK 14–12	US 5–7, 3.75–4.50mm, old UK 9–7	B/1	
fingering	3/14 (or 50/140 Tex)	770	US 3–5, 3.00–3.75mm, old UK 11–9	US 8–9, 5.50–6.00mm, old UK 6–4	C/2	6–7
doubleknit (dk)	4/14 (or 140/140 Tex)	570	US 5–6, 3.75–4.00mm, old UK 9–8		D/3	5–6
aran	8/14	285	US 7–8, 4.50–5.00mm, old UK 7–6			
chunky	12/14	190	US 8–10, 5.00–6.00mm, old UK 6–4			

Roughly, 300–350g (11–12 oz) of the lace weight or 4 ply should make a pullover—thicker yarns will need extra weight for the same garment so, for example, a DK weight pullover might need 500g (18 oz). Amounts below 200g (7 oz) are better for scarves, gloves, baby clothes etc.

18+ wpi is Lace = 2600+ yards per pound

16 wpi is Fingering = 1900 to 2400 yards per pound

14 wpi is Sport = 1200 to 1800 yards per pound

12 wpi is Worsted = 900 to 1200 yards per pound

10 wpi is Bulky = 600 to 800 yards per pound

8 or less wpi is Very Bulky = 400 to 500 yards per pound

basic stitches

In crochet the left hand tensions the yarn and holds the work while the right hand uses the hook. The following show the basic techniques, but use your own methods if you are familiar with them.

Abbreviations

alt	alternate
beg	beginning
bet	between
bl	back of loop
CC	contrasting color
ch	chain
ch sp	chain space
cm	centimeter
cont	continues
dc	double crochet
dec	decrease
fl	front of loop
foll	following/follows
g	gram
hdc	half double crochet
htr	half treble
inc	increase
MC	main color
m	marker
mm	millimeter
patt	pattern
pm	place marker
rem	remaining
rep	repeat
RS	right side
sc	single crochet
sl st	slip stitch
st(s)	stitch(es)
tch	turning chain
tr	treble
WS	wrong side
yo	yarn over

Holding the hook

Hold the hook like a pencil, but lightly so you can maneuver it easily.

Making a slip knot

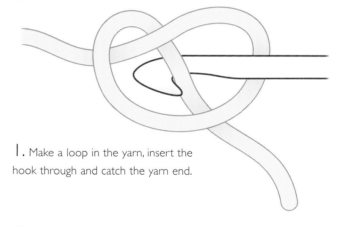

1. Make a loop in the yarn, insert the hook through and catch the yarn end.

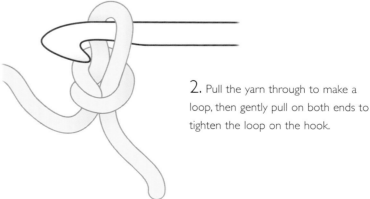

2. Pull the yarn through to make a loop, then gently pull on both ends to tighten the loop on the hook.

Chain stitch

1. With the hook in front of the yarn, take the yarn over the hook from the back to the front and catch the yarn. This basic movement is called yarn over hook.

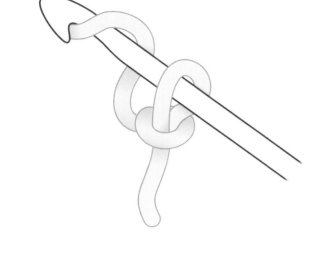

2. Bring the yarn through the loop on the hook to make a new chain loop on the hook.

Slip stitch

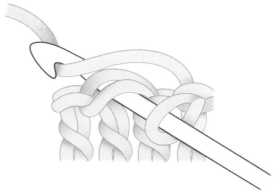

Insert the hook into the stitch and take the yarn over the hook. Draw a new loop through both the stitch and the loop on the hook, ending with one loop on the hook.

Single crochet

1. Insert the hook into the second chain from hook, yarn over hook and pull a loop through.

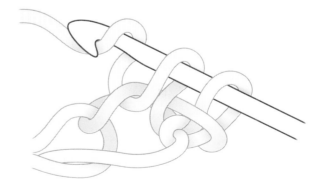

2. Wrap the yarn over the hook pull a loop through both loops. One loop remains on the hook—1 sc made.

Half double

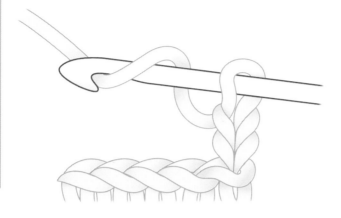

1. Wrap the yarn over the hook and insert into third chain from hook.

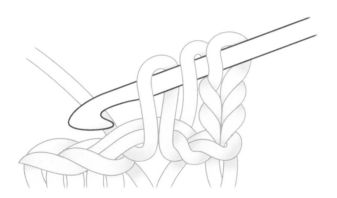

2. Pull a loop through this chain—you now have three loops on the hook. Wrap the yarn over the hook again. Pull through all three loops on the hook.

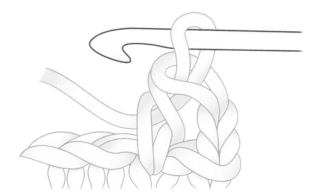

3. One loop remains on the hook—1 hdc made.

double crochet

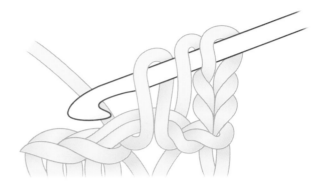

1. Wrap the yarn over the hook and insert into fourth chain from hook. Pull a loop through this chain, you now have three loops on the hook, wrap the yarn over the hook again. Pull through all three loops on the hook.

2. Draw through the first two loops only and wrap the yarn again.

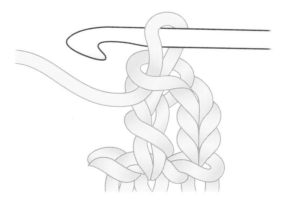

3. Draw through the last two loops on the hook. One loop remains on the hook—1 dc made.

Working longer stitches

Treble, double treble, triple treble, and so on are all worked in the same way as a double, but with one more wrapping of the yarn over the hook for each longer stitch, giving one more step when drawing through two loops at a time.

Here's the number of times to wrap the yarn over the hook when making these longer stitches.

Type of Stitch	Number of times to wrap
Treble	two
Double treble	three
Triple treble	four
Quadruple treble	five

Fastening off

After the last stitch pull another loop through, cut the yarn, and pull the end through.

beads

Beads are seductive! Walking into any bead supply store is like entering another world and one visit to an internet search engine will reveal many sources. Do not forget, however, that if you purchase beads from overseas, you may be charged import duty and tax. It is always good to contact these firms before you buy and ask if they already have a supplier in your own country.

wire

Wire is available in many different thicknesses and gauges, ranging from gauge 8 (the thickest) to gauge 34 (the thinnest). It also comes in different metals and coatings. Enamelled copper wire is less expensive than silver-plated wire. The color of the base wire affects the finished color: pink enamel applied to silver wire looks brighter than the same pink enamel applied to copper, for example.

findings

Findings is a general term used to describe ready-made components such as chains, clasps, brooch bars, and earwires. They are readily available from jewelry suppliers, and craft and hobby stores. Findings come in many different finishes—shiny and matte, antique-effect metallic, and so on. Always choose one that both complements the color of the wire and beads that you are using and the style of the piece. Magnetic clasps make a quick-and-easy fastening for a bracelet—but I never use them on necklaces for safety reasons, as other metallic objects can sometimes be attracted to the magnet.

index

suppliers

Most suppliers required for the projects included in this book may be found at your local craft or yarn shop. For speciality products, check the websites listed here.

YARN SUPPLIERS

Adriafil Yarns
www.adriafil.com for stockists

Anny Blatt
www.annyblatt.com for stockists

Debbie Bliss
www.debbieblissonline.com

Bouton D'or
www.boutondor.com

Coats Craft Rowan Yarns
www.coatscrafts.co.uk

Colinette Yarns
www.colinette.com for stockists

Gedifra
Available from
www.yarnmarket.com

Knitglobal
www.knitglobal.com

Lana Grossa
www.lanagrossa.com for stockists

Lanartus Yarns
www.lanartus.net

Lang Yarns
www.langyarns.ch/en
for stockists

Louisa Harding
www.louisaharding.co.uk

Noro Yarns
www.noroyarns.com
for stockists

Patons Yarns
www.patonsyarns.co.uk

Presencia
www.presenciausa.com
for stockists

RY Classic Yarns
www.ryclassic.com

Sirdar Yarns
www.sirdar.co.uk

South West Trading Company
(SWTC) Yarns
www.soysilk.com

Stef Francis
www.stef-francis.co.uk

Trendsetter Yarns
www.trendsetteryarns.com

Twilleys of Stamford
www.twilleys.co.uk for stockists

Wensleydale Longwool
www.wensleydalelongwoolsheep
shop.co.uk

STOCKISTS

Knitting Fever
www.knittingfever.com

Lets Knit
www.letsknit.com

WEBS
www.yarn.com

Yarn Market
www.yarnmarket.com

WIRE

Scientific Wires
www.wires.co.uk

BAG TRIMMINGS
AND HANDLES

Bags of Handles
www.bagsofhandles.co.uk

U Handbags
www.u-handbag.com

BEADS AND BUTTONS

Beads Direct
www.beadsdirect.co.uk

The Button Company
www.buttoncompany.co.uk

Injabulo
www.injabulo.com

acknowledgments

Another journey, this time with one pin—the crochet hook.

I have enjoyed searching for less well used stitches to incorporate into the designs in this book, and have learnt a lot en route as well. As always my inspirations for design and colors start in my sketch book.

My special thanks must go to Cindy Richards who has faith in my abilities and helps turn dreams into books. Thanks also to all CICO staff in London and to the photographer Paul Bricknall who made the shoot enjoyable and produced good images.

Marie Clayton, my editor, with whom I had a cyber relationship, thank you.
Stylist Sue Rowlands; thank you, the book looks great.
Designer Roger Hammond; thank you. I love the look you have created.

Thank you to all the yarn companies who supported me and special thanks go to Karen and Paul at Pavi yarns who always knew where to find just what I needed; thank you both.

Sian Brown; thank you for your dedication to this book and its timeline and help with patterns, which leads me on to a special thank you to Jenny Shore who I think can read my mind, or at least reads my designs well. Thank you Jenny and thanks for the beautiful craftsmanship you portrayed in the items for the book.

Also to Shiela Grudzinski, owner of my local yarn shop, who again is always there to help, and produced a beautiful piece of work for this book, thank you Shiela.

It has not been a easy year but as always my family are my rock, so to:
My husband Nigel, who still has patience in having a creative wife and is still calm, loving and shares my dreams; thank you darling, I could not do it without you.

James and Emma, my duo in whom I have unmeasurable pride, inspire me, believe in me, and do make life so much fun, thank you both.

Not least Linda, my treasure, who also has utter patience with me and the yarn, beads, looms, wheels, needles, and pins that I seem to surround myself with, and who keeps my home an oasis of utter calm, thank you.

MJH—as always my tomorrows are your gift, thank you.

To all of you who wishing you could, or had, or did—do it.

Take hold of your dream
Catch onto that star
Have faith in yourself
You are what you are.

Chrissie Day